1990

11-14

SOURCES OF CIVILIZATION IN THE WEST

Robert Lee Wolff, *General Editor*

ZEPH STEWART, the editor of this volume, is Professor of Greek and Latin and Master of Lowell House at Harvard University, and the author of numerous articles and reviews on classical subjects.

ALREADY PUBLISHED

THE

ANCIENT
WORLD:

JUSTICE, HEROISM,
AND RESPONSIBILITY

Edited by

Zeph Stewart

PRENTICE-HALL, INC.
Englewood Cliffs, New Jersey

Current printing (last digit):

11 10 9 8 7 6 5

FOREWORD

Hammurabi stands at the beginning of this book and Justinian at its end, some 2300 years later. Hammurabi calls himself "King of Justice," and Justinian declares that the Roman Emperor must show himself as regardful of justice as of triumph in war. The divine tribunal of ancient Egyptian gods deals out justice after death; for Hesiod, the rule of law is what distinguishes man from the animals, who live by the law of the jungle.

The hero Achilles receives the aged King Priam and returns to him the body of Hector. The hero Leonidas and his small band show King Xerxes that his huge Persian armies contain "plenty of combatants but very few warriors." Antigone defies Creon: the heroine thwarts the tyrant and pays due reverence to the divine law, though she dies for it. Aeneas looks with wonder at his new shield: on it the god Vulcan has wrought the whole future history of the great Roman city that Aeneas has not yet founded. For the sophisticated Aristotle, the great-souled man is still in essence a Homeric hero.

Responsibility twines itself like a third golden thread with justice and heroism into the fabric of ancient civilization, from Babylon and Egypt through Greece and Rome. By his selection of these themes and by his choice of passages that illustrate them Professor Stewart has given us an arresting book. His commentary, with the art that conceals art, takes us with brevity, grace, and learning down the centuries and the millennia. For Homer, Pindar, and Catullus we have Professor Stewart's own new and excellent translations. Notice how even familiar passages gain by their new juxtaposition here. How do we relate the Socrates on trial for his life, and surprised that the majority against him is not even bigger, with the Socrates aloft in the basket in the comic think-shop? Why does Horace see Cleopatra as "no craven woman," but Virgil see her as "pale in terror at the menace of death"?

Here are some of the most moving words that human beings have ever written. It is clear that, like Cicero, Professor Stewart believes that literature is the incentive to noble action, but that it is also fun.

Robert Lee Wolff
Coolidge Professor of History
Harvard University

PREFACE

The purpose of this book is to illustrate with a selection of primary texts three central themes in the cultural history of the ancient world. It is not intended in any way as a general anthology of ancient literature or history. In fact many important authors, including some of my own favorites, are not represented. Given the severe limitations of space, my first task was to choose points of reference. I have done so by singling out a special contribution of each major period to European culture: for the ancient Near East it is the growth of a sense of justice and social morality (which has so interested modern western historians), for the Greek world the concept of the hero, and for the Roman world the idea of community responsibility. These are themes which persist and overlap; so although each is emphasized in certain sections, all three run through the whole work with no sharp break between one period and another.

The texts are in most cases substantial selections, not snippets chosen merely to illustrate a theme. They are in every instance important and central ones in the history of ancient thought. In order to achieve some variety within so small a compass much material that would be appropriate has been omitted. I particularly regret the omission of Aeschylus. The introductions to sections and to individual texts are meant to give an historical and literary background, but always in terms of these particular themes. They neglect much that would be included in an historical survey or literary anthology. But with few exceptions (such as Sallust) I have tried to say enough about each author and to include a sufficiently long or typical example of his work to give some idea of him as an individual writer and thinker in the context of his time.

No one who knows Greek and Latin is ever satisfied with translations of them, least of all his own. The choice between different versions has been difficult and perhaps sometimes wrong. In the case of poetry I have used verse translations in certain instances when there was one which seemed to me especially satisfactory.

I shall be most grateful to any user of this book for his criticisms, and especially for suggestions about what might be omitted as least useful or what other selections might be substituted in the event that there should be need for a revised edition.

Acknowledgment with thanks is hereby made to the publishers and individuals who have allowed me to use their copyrighted materials. I am particularly grateful to the Harvard University Press, publishers of the Loeb Classical Library, and to the Oxford University Press.

This is a pleasant opportunity to thank my friend Robert L. Wolff, Coolidge Professor of History at Harvard and an editor of this series, both for the initial suggestion of this book and for generous advice and encouragement along the way. I am, as always, grateful to my wife for her help and to her family, Mr. and Mrs. Robert A. Childers of Earlswood, Surrey, and Mr. and Mrs. Robert C. Barton of Glendalough House, County Wicklow, for provision of hospitable and efficient facilities for my work.

CONTENTS

Part One

THE ANCIENT NEAR EAST

During the last few decades archaeologists and linguists have made startling discoveries in the lands bordering on the Mediterranean. For the historian interested in this area, which is the background of European ancient history, these discoveries have provided new insights into whole periods as well as the illumination of many new details. Perhaps the most important general result has been the realization of how closely interrelated were the lands of the Mediterranean world—and especially those of its eastern sector—in the middle and later centuries of the second millennium before Christ. Between 1600 and 1150 B.C. Hittite kings in what is now central Turkey mention in their documents Greek Achaeans; records from the Nile valley speak of Greek Achaean and possibly Danaan attacks on Egypt; Crete and mainland Greece shared the same form of writing; extensive trade was carried on among all these lands and with the Syrian coast as well; and there is evidence that settlers or traders ventured west to Italy and Sicily. Our nineteenth-century historians were soon converted—by Schliemann's discoveries in Troy, Mycenae, and Tiryns and Evans' later work in Crete—to a belief in the essential historicity of the Homeric poems and of many Greek legends. They still hesitated to accept, however, the general conviction of the ancient Greeks that their own early ties stretched toward the east and south—toward Asia Minor and Egypt. Modern historians continued to feel sure that the Greeks were fairly recent arrivals from the north and that all such legends and accounts were mistaken or misplaced. The discoveries of the last few years have done much to reverse this scepticism, and the myths and legends of classical Greece are treated with increasing respect as accounts which seem ever better confirmed as reflections of fact.

It has been in some ways disconcerting to discover that the mainland Greeks of this "Mycenaean" period were organized in each center around a kind of palace bureaucracy. The system seems to have resembled those centralized regimes of Egypt and Asia which have been so often contrasted with the products of the Greek spirit. It ought not to have been surprising, however, to find such similarities in a world so homogeneous as the eastern Mediterranean in the second millennium B.C. What is really surprising is that out of the intervening dark age of disorganization and destruction the Greeks should have developed, after 800 B.C., into a people of such distinct and independent spirit, while the successive eastern kingdoms remained generally so autocratic and monolithic.

It has been the custom to begin histories of Europe with some account of the ancient Near East. There have been several reasons for doing so. First has been the mere geographical fact that European history began at the eastern edge of Europe. Secondly, the earliest historical civilizations of Europe proper always themselves looked to the Near Eastern kingdoms as their ancient neighbors and sometimes preceptors. Finally, the continually close relationship of the Asiatic and African sides of the Mediterranean with the European side in the Greek and Roman periods made knowledge of the ancient Near East seem important to the understanding of later developments. But until recently it has always seemed clear that the Near East was one thing and Greek (and Roman) civilization quite another, with widely separated and differing backgrounds as well as ideals. It was thought, for example, that no direct contact could have conveyed eastern religious and moral ideas to the Greeks except in the much later period of an expanded Greek world, and eventually through the Jews and Christians. For the later Greeks of Homer and afterwards this traditional judgment may well be true, as will be clear later. But we have now learned from the decipherment of Linear B script that the ancestors of the classical Greeks were one of a great community of nations and shared many common institutions with their eastern neighbors. In what seems therefore more and more to be one world of the third and second millennia B.C., Near Eastern culture has come to have a more genuinely relevant interest for the European historian of today.

The Code of Hammurabi

Scholars have long noted that even in systems which seem to us ruler-ridden and harshly autocratic there were early glimmerings of social justice and of the claims of humanity. The most famous record of enlightened restraint in a monolithic ancient society is the Code promulgated by Hammurabi, king of Babylonia toward 1750 B.C. A copy written on a stone pillar was found in the excavations at Susa in 1901. This energetic monarch created the first extensive empire centered at Babylon, and his proud boast that he had brought peace, order, and prosperity to his domain is confirmed by the numerous documents which have survived from this period. The Code itself contains elements from much earlier times, and its principles continued to be influential in the centuries of changing regimes and peoples which followed in the Mesopotamian area. But for us it represents the most complete written public guarantee of fixed justice in an area close to the beginnings of European civilization. Dealing with all aspects of personal, business, and public life, it establishes rules which differ for different classes, but in which all are given protection and responsibilities and are treated with an obvious attempt at appropriate justice.

The following selections are reprinted from G. R. Driver and J. K. Miles, *The Babylonian Laws*, Vol. II, by permission of the Clarendon Press, Oxford.

§1   If a man has accused a man and has charged him with manslaughter and then has not proved (it against) him, his accuser shall be put to death.

§§3-4   If a man has come forward in a case to bear witness to a felony and then has not proved the statement that he has made, if that case (is) a capital one, that man shall be put to death. If he has come forward to bear witness to (a claim for) corn or money, he shall remain liable for the penalty for that suit.

§5   If a judge has tried a suit, given a decision, caused a sealed tablet to be executed, (and) thereafter varies his judgement, they shall convict that judge of varying (his) judgement and he shall pay twelve-fold the claim in that suit; then they shall remove him from his place on the bench of judges in the assembly, and he shall not (again) sit in judgement with the judges.

§§22-24 If a man has committed robbery and is caught, that man shall be put to death. If the robber is not caught, the man who has been robbed shall formally declare whatever he has lost before a god, and the city and the mayor in whose territory or district the robbery has been committed shall replace whatever he has lost for him. If (it is) the life (of the owner that is lost), the city or the mayor shall pay one maneh of silver to his kinsfolk.

§§55-56 If a man has opened his trench for irrigation (and) has been slack and so has let the water carry away (the soil on) his neighbour's field, he shall pay corn corresponding to (the amount of the crop which) his neighbour (has raised). If a man has released the waters and so has let the waters carry away the works on his neighbour's field, he shall pay 10 GUR of corn for every BUR (of land).

§§122-123 If a man wishes to give silver (or) gold or anything whatsoever to a man for safe custody, he shall show anything whatsoever that he gives to witnesses, he shall draw up a contract and (thus) give (them) for safe custody. If he has given (them) for safe custody without witnesses or a contract and those with whom he gave them contest (them), that case affords no cause of action.

§§159-60 If a man, who has had a gift brought to his father-in-law's house (and) given a bridal gift, has then looked upon another woman and states to his father-in-law 'I will not take thy daughter to wife,' the father of the girl shall take and keep anything that has been brought to him. If a man has had a gift brought to his father-in-law's house (or) has given a bridal gift, and the father of the girl states 'I will not give thee my daughter (in marriage),' he must double everything that has been brought to him and restore (it).

§162 If a man has taken a wife (and) she has borne him sons, and that woman has then gone to (her) fate, her father shall not bring a claim (against him) for dowry; her dowry belongs to her sons.

§§185-86 If a man has taken an infant in adoption (to be called) by his name and brings him up, that adopted child shall not be (re)claimed. If the man has taken the infant in adoption (and), when he has taken it, it persists in searching for its father and its mother, that adopted child shall return to its father's house.

§§206-208 If a man strikes a (free) man in an affray and inflicts a wound on him, that man may swear 'Surely I did not strike (him) wittingly,' and he shall pay the surgeon. If he dies of the striking, he may swear likewise; if (the victim is) a (free) man, he shall pay ½ maneh of silver. If (he is) a villein, he shall pay ⅓ maneh of silver.

§§215-20 If a surgeon has made a deep incision in (the body of) a (free) man with a lancet(?) of bronze and saves the man's life or has opened the caruncle(?) in (the eye of) a man with a lancet (?) of bronze and saves his eye, he shall take 10 shekels of silver. If (the patient is) a villein, he shall take 5 shekels of silver. If (the patient is) the slave of a (free) man, the master of the slave shall give 2 shekels of silver to the surgeon. If the surgeon has made a deep incision in (the body of) a (free) man with a lancet (?) of bronze and causes the man's death or has opened the caruncle(?) in (the eye of) a man and so destroys the man's eye, they shall cut off his fore-hand. If the surgeon has made a deep incision in (the body of) a villein's slave with a lancet(?) of bronze and causes (his) death, he shall replace slave for slave. If he has opened his caruncle (?) with a lancet (?) of bronze and destroys his eye, he shall pay half his price in silver.

*   *   *

(These are) the just laws which Hammurabi the able king has stablished and (thereby) has enabled the land to enjoy stable governance and good rule . . . Let the oppressed man who has a cause go before my statue (called) 'King of Justice' and then have the inscription on my monument read out and hear my precious words, that my monument may make clear (his) cause to him, let him see the law which applies to him, (and) let his heart be set at ease, saying 'The lord Hammurabi, who is a true father to the people, hath now bowed himself down at the word of Marduk his lord and hath fulfilled the earnest desire of Marduk from north to south; he hath gladdened the heart of Marduk his lord, hath brought prosperity to the people for ever, and he hath also given justice to the land.'

The *Book of the Dead*

It has often been noted that the Egyptians differed radically from the classical Greeks and Romans in their concentration on what happens after death. Here too, as in other institutions, the earlier Greeks of the Mycenaean age appear to have more closely resembled their Near Eastern neighbors than their classical descendants. Some of the most striking finds at Mycenae have been the great "bee-hive" tombs, the grave circles, and the death masks of beaten gold. In Egypt the elaborate care of the dead was not a passing phase, however, but a phenomenon continuing from the earliest to the latest times, and it had some extraordinarily creative side-effects. Just as the most impressive monuments and some of the finest art of Egypt—the pyramids, tomb paintings and sculptures, elaborate mummy-wrappings and cases, all the exquisite furniture and ornaments in tomb chambers—resulted from this attention to the aftermath of death, so the most remarkable work in literature was the so-called *Book of the Dead*. This somewhat unsatisfactory but now universally accepted title is given to a diverse collection of prayers, hymns, narratives, incantations, and instructions which were enclosed with the dead person, first in a simpler form as wall carvings in the early royal tombs, later, with a new emphasis on magical detail, on papyrus rolls in more ordinary burials.

The best-known version, the Theban recension which was used in the centuries around 1500 B.C., is exactly contemporary with the greatest development of Mycenaean Greece. Much of the text is difficult and obscure for the modern reader, referring as it does to unfamiliar myths and beliefs and divinities. The object of the writing is to help the dead man gain his soul in the other world, by describing his successful journey and establishment of a new life and by giving him the proper prayers to beg for help and to plead his innocence and purity before a final tribunal. It is this last feature which is of such interest to those who look for the earliest traces of a sense of morality and social justice in the Mediterranean world, for it is clear that the idea of such a general tribunal after death had begun to develop in Egypt perhaps a thousand years before the date of these texts.

It should be noted in what follows that the dead person (N.) himself identified with the god Osiris and that there is more than one trial to undergo, the first being the "weighing of the heart" in the scales with truth.

The following selections are reprinted from E. A. Wallis Budge, *The Book of the Dead,* by arrangement with the Medici Society Ltd., London, and University Books, Inc., New Hyde Park, New York.

A Hymn of Praise to Ra When He Riseth on the Eastern Horizon of Heaven, and to Those Who Are in his Train [from Chapter XV]: Homage to thee, O Heru-Khuti, who art the god Khepera, the self-created. When thou risest on the horizon and sheddest thy beams of light upon the Lands of the South and of the North, thou art beautiful, yea beautiful, and all the gods rejoice when they behold thee, the king of heaven. The goddess, the Lady of the Hour, is established upon thy brow, and she taketh up her place before thee. The god Thoth is stablished in the bows of thy boat to destroy utterly all thy foes. Those who dwell in the Tuat come forth to meet thee, and they bow to the earth in homage as they come towards thee, to look upon thy beautiful Form. And I, N., have come into thy presence, so that I may be with thee, and may behold thy disk every day. Let me not be kept captive by the tomb, and let me not be turned back on my way. Let the members of my body be made new again when I contemplate thy beauties, even as are the members of all thy favoured ones, because I am one of those who worshipped thee upon the earth. Let me arrive in the Land of Eternity, let me enter into the Land of Everlastingness. This, O my lord, behold thou shalt ordain for me.

The Prayer of N. [Chapter XXXB]: My heart, my mother; my heart, my mother! My heart whereby I came into being! May nought stand up to oppose me at my judgment, may there be no opposition to me in the presence of the Chiefs; may there be no parting of thee from me in the presence of him that keepeth the Balance! Thou are my Ka, which dwelleth in my body; the god Khnemu who knitteth together and strengtheneth my limbs. Mayest thou come forth into the place of happiness whither we go. May the Sheniu officials, who make the conditions of the lives of men, not cause my name to stink, and may no lies be spoken against me in the presence of the God.

The Speech of Thoth: Thoth, the judge of right and truth of the Great Company of the Gods who are in the presence of Osiris, saith: Hear ye this judgment. The heart of Osiris hath in very truth been weighed, and his Heart-soul hath borne testimony on his behalf; his heart hath been found right by the trial in the Great Balance. There hath not been found any wickedness in him; he hath not wasted (or stolen) the offerings which have been made in the temples; he hath not committed any evil act; and he hath not set his mouth in motion with words of evil whilst he was upon earth.

Address to the Gods of the Tuat [from Chapter CXXV]: N., [professional description of N.], whose word is truth, saith: Homage to you, O ye gods who dwell in the Hall of Maati. I know you, I know your names. Let me not fall under your knives of slaughter, and bring ye not forward my wickedness to this god in whose following you are.

Let not evil hap come upon me through you. Speak ye the truth concerning me in the presence of Neb-er-tcher, for I have done what is right and just in Egypt. I have not cursed the god, and my evil hap did not come upon him that was king in his day. Homage to you, O ye who dwell in your Hall of Maati, who have nothing false in your bodies, who live upon Truth, who feed yourselves upon Truth in the presence of Horus who dwelleth in his Disk; deliver ye me from Beba, who feedeth upon the livers of the great ones on the day of the Great Judgment. Grant ye that I may come before you, for I have not committed sin, I have done no act of deceit, I have done no evil thing, and I have not borne false witness; therefore let nothing evil be done to me. I have lived upon truth, I have fed upon truth, I have performed the ordinances of men, and the things which gratify the gods. I have propitiated the god by doing his will, I have given bread to the hungry man, and water to him that was athirst, and apparel to the naked man, and a ferry-boat to him that had no boat. I have made propitiatory offerings and given cakes to the gods, and the "things which appear at the word" to the Spirits. Deliver then ye me, protect then ye me, and make ye no report against me in the presence of the Great God. I am pure in respect of my mouth, and I am clean in respect of my hands; therefore let it be said unto me by those who shall behold me: "Come in peace, Come in peace."

Hymn to Osiris [Chapter CLXXXV]: Homage to thee, O thou Holy God, thou almighty and beneficent being, thou Prince of Eternity, who dwellest in thy abode in the Sektet Boat, whose risings are manifold in the Atet Boat, unto whom praises are rendered in heaven and upon earth. Peoples and nations exalt thee, and the awe of thy terror is in the hearts of men, and Spirit-souls, and the dead . . . I have come unto thee. Truth is in my heart, and in my breast is neither craft nor guile. Grant thou that I may have my being among the living, and that I may sail up and down the river among those who are in thy following.

Ikhnaton's Hymn to the Sun-god

Today the best known event in Egyptian religious history is a most untypical and short-lived development under Amenophis (Amenhotep) IV and his immediate successors toward 1375 B.C. In a revolutionary rejection of traditional polytheism he devoted himself to the worship of the Sun-god conceived under a new name, Aton (or Aten), as the disk of the sun. He built a new capital, Akhetaton, "Horizon of Aton," at modern Tell-el-Amarna, changed his own name to Ikhnaton (or Akhenaten), "He who is beneficial to Aton," and even tried, it seems, to extend the worship of the new divinity beyond his domain. This first example of monotheism and universalism in the ancient world has excited much interest and speculation in recent times. It is therefore important to note that the new religion appears to have had no special moral content, quite unlike the monotheism of the Hebrews. In the tombs of nobles cut in the cliffs behind Ikhnaton's city have been found hymns and other evidence of the new worship inscribed on the walls. The king and his court seem to have limited themselves to the contemplation and praise of the power and beauty of their divinity. In many respects the longest and most important hymn resembles the many other Egyptian hymns to the traditional Sun-god.

The following selections are reprinted with the permission of Charles Scribner's Sons from the "Royal Hymn to the Sun-god" of *The Dawn of Conscience,* pp. 281-286, by James Henry Breasted (Copyright © 1933 James Henry Breasted; renewal copyright © 1961 Charles Breasted, James Breasted, Jr., and Astrid Breasted Hormann).

Universal Splendour and Power of Aton

Thou dawnest beautifully in the horizon of the sky,
O living Aton who wast the Beginning of life!
When thou didst rise in the eastern horizon,
Thou didst fill every land with thy beauty.
Thou art beautiful, great, glittering, high over every land,
Thy rays, they encompass the lands, even to the end of all that thou hast made.
Thou art Re, and thou penetratest to the very end of them;
Thou bindest them for thy beloved son (the Pharaoh).
Though thou art far away, thy rays are upon earth;
Though thou art in the faces of men, thy footsteps are unseen.

Day and Man

Bright is the earth when thou risest in the horizon;
When thou shinest as Aton by day
Thou drivest away the darkness.
When thou sendest forth thy rays,
The Two Lands (Egypt) are in daily festivity.
Men waken and stand upon their feet

When thou hast raised them up.
Their limbs bathed, they take their clothing,
Their arms uplifted in adoration to thy dawning.
Then in all the world they do their work.

Day and the Animals and Plants

All cattle rest upon their pasturage,
The trees and the plants flourish,
The birds flutter in their marshes,
Their wings uplifted in adoration to thee.
All the antelopes dance upon their feet,
All creatures that fly or alight,
They live when thou hast shone upon them.

Day and the Waters

The barques sail up-stream and down-stream alike.
Every highway is open because thou dawnest.
The fish in the river leap up before thee.
Thy rays are in the midst of the great green sea.

Universal Creation

How manifold are thy works!
They are hidden before men,
O sole God, beside whom there is no other.
Thou didst create the earth according to thy heart.
While thou wast alone:
Even men, all herds of cattle and the antelopes;
All that are upon the earth,
That go about upon their feet;
They that are on high,
That fly with their wings.
The highland countries, Syria and Kush,
And the land of Egypt;
Thou settest every man into his place,
Thou suppliest their necessities,
Every one has his food,
And his days are reckoned.
The tongues are diverse in speech,
Their forms likewise and their skins are distinguished,
For thou makest different the strangers.

Revelation to the King

. . . .

There is no other that knoweth thee
Save thy son Ikhnaton.
Thou hast made him wise
In thy designs and in thy might.

Universal Maintenance

The world subsists in thy hand,
Even as thou hast made them.
When thou hast risen they live,
When thou settest they die;
For thou art length of life of thyself,
Men live through thee . . .
The eyes of men see beauty
Until thou settest.
All labour is put away
When thou settest in the west.
When thou risest again
[Thou] makest [every hand] to flourish for the king
And [prosperity] is in every foot,
Since thou didst establish the world,
And raise them up for thy son,
Who came forth from thy flesh,
The king of Upper and Lower Egypt,
Living in Truth, Lord of the Two Lands,
Nefer-khepru-Re, Wan-Re (Ikhnaton),
Son of Re, living in Truth, lord of diadems,
Ikhnaton, whose life is long;
(And for) the chief royal wife, his beloved,
Mistress of the Two Lands, Nefer-nefru-Aton, Nofretete,
Living and flourishing for ever and ever.

David and Bathsheba

There was an enormous difference between Ikhnaton's conception of his god, all-powerful and all-moving but somehow distant and impersonal, and the god of the Hebrews. The peculiarly intimate relationship of their divinity to his "prophets," those who knew his intent, and to the moral life of the rulers and nation is nowhere more clearly and dramatically conceived than in the story of David and Bathsheba. The familiar account needs no commentary. David had united the north and south of Israel toward 1000 B.C., capturing Jerusalem, and establishing his capital there. Successful wars had given him power and prosperity. His general, Joab, was campaigning against the neighboring state of Ammon.

The passage is from the Second Book of Samuel, XI-XII:12 (King James Version).

And it came to pass, after the year was expired, at the time when kings go forth to battle, that David sent Joab, and his servants with him, and all Israel; and they destroyed the children of Ammon, and besieged Rabbah. But David tarried still at Jerusalem.

And it came to pass in an eveningtide, that David arose from off his bed, and walked upon the roof of the king's house. And from the roof he saw a woman washing herself; and the woman was very beautiful to look upon. And David sent and enquired after the woman. And one said, Is not this Bathsheba, the daughter of Eliam, the wife of Uriah the Hittite? And David sent messengers, and took her; and she came in unto him, and he lay with her; for she was purified from her uncleanliness. And she returned unto her house. And the woman conceived, and sent and told David, and said, I am with child.

And David sent to Joab, saying, Send me Uriah the Hittite. And Joab sent Uriah to David. And when Uriah was come unto him, David demanded of him how Joab did, and how the people did, and how the war prospered. And David said to Uriah, Go down to thy house, and wash thy feet. And Uriah departed out of the king's house, and there followed him a mess of meat from the king. But Uriah slept at the door of the king's house with all the servants of his lord, and went not down to his house. And when they had told David, saying, Uriah went not down unto his house, David said unto Uriah, Camest thou not from thy journey? why then didst thou not go down unto thine house? And Uriah said unto David, The ark, and Israel, and Judah, abide in tents; and my lord Joab, and the servants of my lord, are encamped in the open fields; shall I then go into mine house, to eat and to drink, and to lie with my wife? as thou livest, and as thy soul liveth, I will not do this thing. And David said to Uriah, Tarry here today also, and tomorrow I will let thee depart. So Uriah abode in Jerusalem that day, and the morrow. And when David had called him, he did eat and drink before him; and he made him drunk. And at even he went out to lie on his bed with the servants of his lord, but went not down to his house.

And it came to pass in the morning, that David wrote a letter to Joab, and sent it by the hand of Uriah. And he wrote in the letter, saying, Set ye Uriah in the forefront of the hottest battle, and retire ye from him, that he may be smitten, and die. And it came to pass, when Joab observed the city, that he assigned Uriah unto a place where he knew that valiant men were. And the men of the city went out, and fought with Joab. And there fell some of the people of the servants of David; and Uriah the Hittite died also.

Then Joab sent and told David all the things concerning the war; and charged the messenger, saying, When thou hast made an end of telling the matters of the war unto the king, and if so be that the king's wrath arise, and he say unto thee, Wherefore approached ye so nigh unto the city when ye did fight? knew ye not that they would shoot from the wall? who smote Abimelech the son of Jerubbesheth? did not a woman cast a piece of a millstone upon him from the wall, that he died in Thebez? why went ye nigh the wall? then say thou, Thy servant Uriah the Hittite is dead also.

So the messenger went, and came and showed David all that Joab had sent him for. And the messenger said unto David, Surely the men prevailed against us, and came out unto us into the field, and we were upon them even unto the entering of the gate. And the shooters shot from off the wall upon thy servants; and some of the king's servants be dead, and thy servant Uriah the Hittite is dead also. Then David said unto the messenger, Thus shalt thou say unto Joab, Let not this thing displease thee, for the sword devoureth one as well as another; make thy battle more strong against the city, and overthrow it and encourage thou him. And when the wife of Uriah heard that Uriah her husband was dead, she mourned for her husband. And when the mourning was past, David sent and fetched her to his house, and she became his wife, and bare him a son.

But the thing that David had done displeased the Lord. And the Lord sent Nathan unto David. And he came unto him, and said unto him, There were two men in one city; the one rich, and the other poor. The rich man had exceeding many flocks and herds. But the poor man had nothing, save one little ewe lamb, which he had bought and nourished up; and it grew up together with him, and with his children; it did eat of his own meat, and drank of his own cup, and lay in his bosom, and was unto him as a daughter. And there came a traveller unto the rich man, and he spared to take of his own flock and of his own herd, to dress for the warfaring man that was come unto him; but took the poor man's lamb, and dressed it for the man that was come to him. And David's anger was greatly kindled against the man; and he said to Nathan, As the Lord liveth, the man that hath done this thing shall surely die; and he shall restore the lamb fourfold, because he did this thing, and because he had no pity.

And Nathan said to David, Thou art the man. Thus saith the Lord God of Israel, I anointed thee king over Israel, and I delivered thee out of the hand of Saul; and I gave thee thy master's house, and thy master's wives into thy bosom, and gave thee the house of Israel and of Judah; and if that had been too little, I would moreover have given unto thee such and such things. Wherefore hast thou despised the commandment of the Lord, to do evil in his sight? thou hast killed Uriah the Hittite with the sword, and hast taken his wife to be thy wife, and hast slain him with the sword of the children of Ammon. Now therefore the sword shall never depart from thine house; because thou hast despised me, and hast taken the wife of Uriah the Hittite to be thy wife. Thus saith the Lord, Behold, I will raise up evil against thee out of thine own house, and I will take thy wives before thine eyes, and give them unto thy neighbour, and he shall lie with thy wives in the sight of this sun. For thou didst it secretly; but I will do this thing before all Israel, and before the sun.

Part Two

THE GREEK HEROIC AGE

In the years following 1200 B.C. the Mycenaean civilization of the Greek mainland, and after it the remaining Minoan civilization of Crete, were disrupted and destroyed. The Dorians, a group of northern Greeks who had remained outside the ambit of Mycenaean culture, appear to have slowly pressed south in raids, destroying the palaces and citadels as they moved. They settled finally in the southernmost part of the Greek peninsula, on the adjacent islands, and on Crete. Gone were the great centers of power, the organized trade, gone even the writing, which had been limited apparently to a few professionals and used for purposes mainly of accounts and inventories. There followed some three centuries of a dark age, when the Greeks, cut off from contact with other lands and without a centralizing force at home, made as it were a new beginning.

The Greece which emerged from this period was the Greece which seems familiar to us as the source of much that remains vital in our own civilization. Toward 800 B.C. writing was adopted from the Phoenicians, a literature began to evolve, overseas trade was resumed, and the separate city-states began to divide Greece into their spheres of influence. The previous culture might seem forgotten, so remote and alien was it from the new world which was developing. But it was far from forgotten, merely transformed. During the dark age, among the Achaean refugees of the Mycenaean world who crowded into Athens (itself bypassed by the Dorians) and who crossed the Aegean to the Ionian shore of Asia Minor, there were preserved in narrative songs the exploits of the earlier age. They were neither written down—there was no writing —nor memorized, but passed from one generation of bards to another, each singer composing anew for each recitation the story as he had learned it. In the course of such transmission there were no doubt embroideries and transfers and combinations of figures and events, while in succeeding decades new details were added from more recent times, and the picture became composite and full of anachronisms. But the evolution of formulae within the metrical pattern did much to preserve some things unchanged. As a first result of the introduction of writing two long poems of this kind were written down and became the foundation stones of western literature, the *Iliad* and the *Odyssey*.

The *Iliad* is essentially a simple story, the account of an incident during a great Achaean siege of Troy (a city which commanded the Dardanelles and the northwest plain of the Asia Minor coast). Achilles, the foremost fighter of the Achaeans, his dignity injured by the taking back of a woman given him from the spoils of local raids, withdraws to his own camp on the shore and refuses to fight. In anger at Agamemnon, the commander of the expedition who had slighted him, he threatens to return home or to repulse the Trojans only when they attack his own encampment. Unyielding to pleas even when the Trojans press hard upon the beached Achaean ships, he at last allows his friend Patroclus to wear his armor and drive back the enemy. Patroclus is killed by the Trojan hero Hector. Achilles in a fury of remorse forgets his grievance, re-enters the conflict, and kills Hector.

Such is the simple tale. But it is told with such a wealth of background and digression and detail that the sweeping canvas pictures a whole world, of gods as well as of men. To later educated Greeks Homer, as they called the author of the *Iliad* and *Odyssey*, represented the fountainhead of all knowledge and standards, not merely of warfare and conduct and theology, but of technical skills as well, and especially of the art of communication. In him one should look for the best narrative style, the most deft characterization, the most effective persuasion, the proper hymnology. In him one found not only the standards of truth and noble action, but also the right words with which to express them. And later, when a new morality and religious sense appeared, it was against Homer that its leaders pointedly reacted. It would be hard to overestimate the importance of the Homeric poems in the literate culture of Greece and indeed of Europe in general. Whole attitudes toward life have been affected, for example, by Achilles' momentous decision, in the eighteenth book of the *Iliad,* to choose a life short but glorious instead of a longer one without honor.

The *Iliad:* The Ransoming of Hector

There is a peculiar magic in the *Iliad* which has accounted for its tremendous influence and undying popularity. Although it is a product and reflection of an heroic age—an age of battles and kings and nobles and bards and fixed traditions of conduct—the *Iliad* is more than just a picture of military nobility. In the figure of Achilles it draws an heroic character who eventually transcends his own inherited traditions of heroism and dignity and becomes, first in his passion of vengeful grief for Patroclus and then in his unbelievably gentle humanity with Priam, a divinely endowed figure acting beyond the usual expectation of contemporary society. For the Greeks he set a special standard of the heroic which was to find an echo in many different situations and aspects of their life and thought.

At the very end of the *Iliad*, after his magnificent burial of Patroclus, Achilles continues in his grief and anger to abuse Hector's dead body, dragging it by the feet behind his chariot through the dust. But the gods take pity and keep stain and corruption from the corpse and decide at last to arrange for Hector's father, Priam, the aged king of Troy, to ransom the body of his son for burial. Achilles is told of the decision by his goddess mother, and a divine messenger is sent to Priam. The old man takes rich presents from his store-chests and despite the anguished entreaties of his wife and household sets out in the night toward the enemy camp across the plain, with his charioteer as sole companion. The god Hermes meets them in disguise and brings them to the camp. The ensuing scene between implacable enemies, Achaean and Trojan, the father petitioning the killer of his son, gentle speech between fierce fighters, is a moment seldom equalled in western literature for its understanding of the realities of human life and the depth of human sympathy.

The following passage is from the *Iliad*, 24.448-691, translated by the editor.

But when they had come to the shelter of Peleus' son,
the lofty shelter which the Myrmidons had built for their king,
hewing beams of pine—and they had roofed it over
with shaggy thatch which they gathered from the meadows;
and around it they made for their king a great court-yard

with close-set hedgepoles; its gate was secured by a single bar
of pine, which three Achaeans could drive home in its socket,
and three could draw back the great bolt of the gate
(three of the others, that is, but Achilles could close it alone)—
at that point fleet Hermes opened the gate for the old man,
and brought in the magnificent gifts for the swift-footed son of Peleus,
and stepping down to the ground from the chariot, he spoke:
"Old sir, I that have come to you am an immortal god,
Hermes. My father sent me to guide you on your way.
But now I shall go back again, and shall not appear
before the eyes of Achilles. It would be good cause for anger,
that an immortal god should openly consort with mortals.
But you go in, and clasp the knees of the son of Peleus,
and in the name of his father and of his fair-haired mother entreat him,
and of his son, that you may stir his spirit within him."
   Thus Hermes spoke, and departed to high Olympus,
and Priam lept down to the ground from his chariot;
he left Idaeus behind there—he stayed and guarded
the horses and mules—but the old man made straight for the dwelling
where Achilles, beloved of Zeus, was sitting. Himself
he found, but his companions were sitting elsewhere. Two only,
the warrior Automedon and Alcimus, scion of Ares,
were busy about him. He had just finished now with his meal,
with eating and drinking, and the table was still standing by him.
Unseen by them tall Priam entered, and standing close by,
he clasped Achilles' knees in his arms, and kissed his hands,
those hands that were dread and man-slaying and had killed his many sons.
Just as when deep disaster closes in on someone who in his own land
has killed a man and has fled to a country of others,
to a rich man's house, and those who behold him are filled with wonder,
so Achilles wondered when he saw godlike Priam,
and the others wondered too, and looked at one another.
Now Priam addressed him, however, with words of entreaty:
"Achilles, like to the gods, remember your own father,
whose age is the same as mine, on the sad threshold of old age.
Those who dwell about perhaps are mistreating him,
and there is no one to keep him from destruction and ill.
But he surely, as long as he hears that you are alive,
rejoices in his heart, and has hope from day to day
that he will see his beloved son coming back from Troy.
But I, I am utterly ill-fated, for I had sons, the noblest
that were in broad Troy, but not one of them, I say, is left me.
Fifty there were, when the sons of the Achaeans came—
nineteen were born from the womb of a single mother,
the others women of the palace bore to me—

of all these has raging Ares broken the strength of their knees;
and the one that was alone left to me, who preserved the city and the people,
him, Hector, have you now slain as he was defending his homeland.
For his sake have I come now to the ships of the Achaeans,
to ransom him from you, and I bring gifts without number.
Achilles, I beg you, have regard for the gods, and pity me,
remembering your own father. And yet more pitiful am I:
I have endured such a thing as no other earthly mortal has ever endured,
to stretch out my hand to the slayer of my sons."
     Thus he spoke, and in the other he awakened grief for his father.
Taking his hand, he put the old man gently from him,
and the two of them with their memories, the one for man-slaying Hector
was weeping bitterly as he huddled before Achilles' feet,
and Achilles was weeping, now for his father, and then again
for Patroclus. And their lament sounded through the house.
But when glorious Achilles had taken his fill of lamenting
and had put desire of it from his mind and body,
at once he rose from his chair, and raised up the old man by his hand,
having pity on his gray head and gray beard,
and addressing him he spoke winged words:
"Ah, unhappy man, many are the evils which you have endured.
How did you dare to come alone to the ships of the Achaeans,
and before my eyes, since it is I who have slain
your many valiant sons? Your heart is of iron.
But come now, sit down upon a chair, and we shall let our sorrows
lie quietly in our hearts, despite our pain.
For there is no profit in chill lamentation.
So it is that the gods have spun the thread for unhappy mortals—
to live in sorrow, while they themselves are without troubles.
Two urns are set by the threshold of Zeus,
of gifts that he gives, one of evil, and the other of blessings.
To whomever Zeus, who delights in thunder, gives a mingled lot,
that man meets sometimes with ill, sometimes with good;
but to whomever he gives from the evil one, him he makes an outcast,
and a dread hunger drives him over the bright earth,
and he wanders honored neither of gods nor mortals.
So too to Peleus did the gods give glorious gifts
from his birth, for he excelled all men
in prosperity and wealth, and he was king over the Myrmidons,
and to him, who was but a mortal, they gave a goddess as his wife;
but upon him too the god brought evil, for never
was there born in his halls a generation of princely sons,
but he had one son only, who is doomed to an early death, and no care
do I give him as he grows old, since far, far from my own land
I abide here in the Troad, bringing sorrows on you and your children.

And of you, old sir, we hear of your prosperity in time past,
how of all that Macar's stronghold, Lesbos, encloses from the sea,
and Phrygia in the upland, and the boundless Hellespont,
over all these you were lord, old sir, by your wealth and your children.
But from the time when the heavenly gods brought upon you this affliction,
always now about your city there are battles and slayings of men.
But take heart, and do not mourn without ceasing,
for it will avail you nothing to grieve for your son,
nor yet will you bring him back to life; before that you will have some other
    sorrow."
     In answer to him spoke the old man, godlike Priam:
"Do not, beloved of Zeus, seat me yet upon a chair, so long as Hector
lies uncared-for among the shelters, but quickly
give him back, that my eyes may look on him; and you take the ransom we
    bring,
which is great. May you have joy in it, and come again
to your native land; for from the first you spared me my life,
to go on living and to look on the light of the sun."
     With an angry glance from beneath his brows spoke to him swift-footed
    Achilles:
"Provoke me no more, old sir. I have in mind of myself
to give back to you Hector. For from Zeus there came to me a messenger,
indeed my mother who bore me, daughter of the old man of the sea;
and you too, Priam, I know in my heart—it doesn't escape me—
that some god led you to the swift ships of the Achaeans.
For no mortal, however young and strong he be, would dare to come
into the encampment. For he could neither pass through the watch
nor easily thrust back the bar of our gateway.
Therefore, old sir, stir up my heart no more amid my sorrows,
for fear that I may spare not even you in our shelters,
suppliant though you are, and may sin against the ordinances of Zeus."
     Thus, he spoke, and the old man was frightened, and obeyed him.
Like a lion the son of Peleus sprang forth from the house,
not alone, for with him followed two henchmen,
the warrior Automedon and Alcimus, they whom most of all
Achilles honored among his companions, after the dead Patroclus.
These then released from their harness the horses and mules
and led the herald indoors, the old king's crier,
and gave him a chair to sit on; then from the smooth-polished wagon
they lifted the countless ransom for the head of Hector.
But they left behind there two heavy cloaks and a fine-woven tunic
in which Achilles could wrap the dead body for its homeward journey.
Achilles called to his serving-women to wash and anoint the body,
taking it to a place apart, that Priam not have sight of his son,
for fear that he not restrain his anger in his grief,

if he should have sight of his son, and Achilles' own wrath be stirred,
and he slay him, and sin against the ordinances of Zeus.
When the serving-women had washed the body and anointed it with oil
and wrapped him in a fair cloak and a tunic,
then Achilles himself lifted him and laid him upon a litter,
and his comrades with him lifted it on to the smooth-polished wagon.
And then he groaned, and called on his beloved companion by name:
"Be not angry with me, Patroclus, if you hear
even in the house of Hades that I have given back great Hector
to his dear father, since the ransom he has given is not unworthy,
and to you too will be given from it all that is fitting."

Thus spoke noble Achilles, and went back into the shelter,
and sat upon the richly-wrought seat from which he had risen,
by the inner wall, and he spoke to Priam, saying:
"Your son, old sir, is given back to you just as you asked it;
he lies upon a bier, and at daybreak as you take him away
you yourself shall see him. But now let us take thought of supper.
For even fair-tressed Niobe took thought of food,
though her twelve children had perished in her halls,
six daughters and six valiant sons in their prime.
The sons Apollo slew with shafts from his silver bow,
being angry with Niobe, and the daughters the archer Artemis,
since Niobe had matched herself with fair-cheeked Leto,
saying that the goddess had borne but two, while she was the mother of many.
And so they, though but two, destroyed them all.
For nine days they lay in their blood, for there was no one
to bury them; for the son of Cronus had turned the people to stones;
but on the tenth day the heavenly gods buried them.
And Niobe took thought of food, when she was weary with weeping.
And now somewhere among the rocks, in the lonely mountains,
on Sipylus, where they say there are resting-places of goddesses,
of nymphs who move in swift dance by the waters of Achelous,
there in stony silence she broods over her sorrows sent by the gods.
Come then, let the two of us likewise, noble old sir, take thought
of food; at a later time you will make lament for your beloved son,
when you have brought him back into Ilium: mourned will he be with many
    tears."

Thus spoke swift Achilles, and sprang up, and a white-fleeced sheep
he slew, and his companion skinned it and made it ready for cooking,
and expertly sliced it in pieces and spitted them,
and roasted all carefully and drew them from the spits.
And Automedon took bread and set it out on the table
in fair baskets, but Achilles divided the meat.
So they put forth their hands to the good things ready before them.

When they had put aside their desire for food and drink,

then Priam, son of Dardanus, looked with wonder at Achilles,
how tall he was and comely: he was like the gods to look on;
and at Priam, son of Dardanus, did Achilles marvel,
as he beheld his valiant looks and listened to his words.
But when they had taken their fill of gazing one upon the other,
the old man, godlike Priam, was the first to speak:
"Show me my bed now quickly, beloved of Zeus, that soon
we may go to our rest and take pleasure in sweet sleep.
For my eyes have not once closed beneath my eyelids
since my son lost his life at your hands,
but I have been endlessly weeping, and brooding over my countless sorrows,
wallowing in the filth in my court-yard enclosure.
Now have I tasted food and have let the flaming wine
pass down my throat. Till now I had tasted nothing."
    He spoke, and Achilles told his companions and the serving-women
to set bedsteads beneath the shelter of the porch and on them
to lay fine purple underbedding, and to spread blankets above,
and on these to put fleecy robes as a cover.
So the serving-women went from the hall with torches in their hands,
and busily made two beds with all speed.
Then spoke bitterly swift-footed Achilles to Priam:
"Outside you must sleep, old sir, my friend, for fear that one of the Achaeans
come to take counsel with me; for they are ever at my side
sitting and taking counsel, as they ought.
If such a one were to catch sight of you in the swift black night,
he would tell it at once to Agamemnon, shepherd of the host,
and there would then be delay in the ransoming of the body.
But come, tell me this, and say exactly
how many days you intend to make a funeral for goodly Hector,
that I may stay quiet myself, and hold back the host."
    The old man, godlike Priam, answered him, saying:
"If you are willing to let me make a full funeral for goodly Hector,
then this is the way, Achilles, that you could let me have my wish:
You know how we are pent up in the city, and wood is far away
to fetch from the mountain, and the Trojans are filled with fear.
Nine days we shall lament for him in our halls,
and on the tenth shall we make his funeral, and the people feast,
and on the eleventh shall we heap up a grave-barrow for him,
and on the twelfth, if we must, shall we do battle."
    Then in answer to him spoke swift-footed goodly Achilles:
"This shall all be, aged Priam, exactly as you would have it:
I shall hold off the attack for as long as you ask me."
    Thus he spoke, and took the old man's right arm
at the wrist, so that his heart would not be fearful.
So two of them slept outside the house in the shelter of the porch,

Priam and the herald, both men of deep counsel:
but Achilles slept in an inner room of the strong-built shelter,
and by his side lay fair-cheeked Briseis.
   Now all the rest of gods and men, lords of chariots,
slumbered the whole night through in bondage to soft sleep,
but upon fleet Hermes sleep could not lay hold,
as he pondered how he might guide from the ships
king Priam unseen by the faithful guards of the gates.
He stood above his head and spoke to him, saying:
"Old sir, you have no thought of evil then, that you still sleep on
in the midst of your enemies, now that Achilles has spared you.
Indeed you have ransomed your son and have given a great price for him,
but thrice as much for your life would they have to pay,
your sons whom you left behind, if by any chance Agamemnon,
son of Atreus, learn of your presence, or the Achaean host find out."
   Thus he spoke, and the old man was filled with fear, and wakened his herald,
And Hermes put harnesses on the horses and mules,
and himself drove them lightly through the camp. And no man knew of their
      going.

Hesiod: *Works and Days*

   The Homeric poems were not the only product of the new Greek
beginnings. Two works, and fragments of others, have come down
to us under the name of Hesiod. Although written in the same
meter and formulaic language, this poetry with its distinctly personal tone and educative interest is quite unlike the impersonal
narrative of Homeric epic. Its subject matter too is different, including aspects of man, nature, and the divine that are largely
missing in Homer. Hesiod, who had apparently lost some inherited
property to a scheming brother, Perses, is deeply concerned with the
meaning of justice in nature and human life and with such questions as the necessity of work, the source of evil, and the relation of
the human to the divine. The *Works and Days* takes its name from
sections describing the work to be done by a farmer in each season
and the supposed usefulness of certain days of the month. It becomes in its later parts a kind of farmers' almanac and a guide
to proverbial superstitions. And indeed it represents throughout
the traditional thought of landsmen about nature, the gods, and
man, just as Homer represents another traditional inheritance.

But Hesiod, like Homer, went far beyond his tradition, and the opening passages reveal the earliest Greek attempt to rationalize and bring into order certain important moral issues, to set the present human existence into some sort of context of history and of divine intent, and to make a distinction between man and the beasts about him. It was an heroic attempt, the first of many, not altogether consistent or even clear. The tale of the hawk and the nightingale, however, left so ambiguously unexplained at the moment, is decisively interpreted in the closing lines of the selection.

For the Greeks Hesiod was probably the most influential author after Homer. In this first part of the *Works and Days* his conviction of the essential rational justice of the present divine order under Zeus is as clear as in his other work, the *Theogony*, on the history of the gods. In spite of occasional notes of pessimism, which give a strangely variegated tone to his poem, Hesiod's striking picture of the two cities is one of the most moving affirmations we possess of the blessings of social justice.

The following selection from *Works and Days*, 27-280, translated by H. G. Evelyn White, is reprinted by permission of the publishers from Loeb Classical Library, *Hesiod, the Homeric Hymns, and Homerica*, Cambridge, Mass.: Harvard University Press.

Perses, lay up these things in your heart, and do not let that Strife who delights in mischief hold your heart back from work, while you peep and peer and listen to the wrangles of the court-house. Little concern has he with quarrels and courts who has not a year's victuals laid up betimes, even that which the earth bears, Demeter's grain. When you have got plenty of that, you can raise disputes and strive to get another's goods. But you shall have no second chance to deal so again: nay, let us settle our dispute here with true judgement which is of Zeus and is perfect. For we had already divided our inheritance, but you seized the greater share and carried it off, greatly swelling the glory of our bribe-swallowing lords who love to judge such a cause as this. Fools! They know not how much more the half is than the whole, nor what great advantage there is in mallow and asphodel.

For the gods keep hidden from men the means of life. Else you would easily do work enough in a day to supply you for a full year even without working; soon would you put away your rudder over the smoke, and the fields worked by ox and sturdy mule would run to waste. But Zeus in the anger of his heart hid it, because Prometheus the crafty deceived him; therefore he planned sorrow and mischief against men. He hid fire; but that the noble son of Iapetus stole again for men from

Zeus the counsellor in a hollow fennel-stalk, so that Zeus who delights in thunder did not see it. But afterwards Zeus who gathers the clouds said to him in anger:

"Son of Iapetus, surpassing all in cunning, you are glad that you have outwitted me and stolen fire—a great plague to you yourself and to men that shall be. But I will give men as the price for fire an evil thing in which they may all be glad of heart while they embrace their own destruction."

So said the father of men and gods, and laughed aloud. And he bade famous Hephaestus make haste and mix earth with water and to put in it the voice and strength of human kind, and fashion a sweet, lovely maiden-shape, like to the immortal goddesses in face; and Athene to teach her needlework and the weaving of the varied web; and golden Aphrodite to shed grace upon her head and cruel longing and cares that weary the limbs. And he charged Hermes the guide, the Slayer of Argus, to put in her a shameless mind and a deceitful nature.

So he ordered. And they obeyed the lord Zeus the son of Cronos. Forthwith the famous Lame God moulded clay in the likeness of a modest maid, as the son of Cronos purposed. And the goddess bright-eyed Athene girded and clothed her, and the divine Graces and queenly Persuasion put necklaces of gold upon her, and the rich-haired Hours crowned her head with spring flowers. And Pallas Athene bedecked her form with all manner of finery. Also the Guide, the Slayer of Argus, contrived within her lies and crafty words and a deceitful nature at the will of loud thundering Zeus, and the Herald of the gods put speech in her. And he called this woman Pandora, because all they who dwelt on Olympus gave each a gift, a plague to men who eat bread.

But when he had finished the sheer, hopeless snare, the Father sent glorious Argus-Slayer, the swift messenger of the gods, to take it to Epimetheus as a gift. And Epimetheus did not think on what Prometheus had said to him, bidding him never take a gift of Olympian Zeus, but to send it back for fear it might prove to be something harmful to men. But he took the gift, and afterwards, when the evil thing was already his, he understood.

For ere this the tribes of men lived on earth remote and free from ills and hard toil and heavy sicknesses which bring the Fates upon men; for in misery men grow old quickly. But the woman took off the great lid of the jar with her hands and scattered all these and her thought caused sorrow and mischief to men. Only Hope remained there in an unbreakable home within under the rim of the great jar, and did not fly out at the door; for ere that, the lid of the jar stopped her, by the will of Aegis-holding Zeus who gathers the clouds. But the rest, countless plagues, wander amongst men; for earth is full of evils and the sea is full. Of themselves diseases come upon men continually by day and by night, bringing mischief to mortals silently; for wise Zeus took away speech from them. So is there no way to escape the will of Zeus.

Or if you will, I will sum you up another tale well and skilfully— and do you lay it up in your heart,—how the gods and mortal men sprang from one source.

First of all the deathless gods who dwell on Olympus made a golden race of mortal men who lived in the time of Cronos when he was reigning in heaven. And they lived like gods without sorrow of heart, remote and free from toil and grief: miserable age rested not on them; but with legs and arms never failing they made merry with feasting beyond the reach of all evils. When they died, it was as though they were overcome with sleep, and they had all good things; for the fruitful earth unforced bare them fruit abundantly and without stint. They dwelt in ease and peace upon their lands with many good things, rich in flocks and loved by the blessed gods.

But after the earth had covered this generation—they are called pure spirits dwelling on the earth, and are kindly, delivering from harm, and guardians of mortal men; for they roam everywhere over the earth, clothed in mist and keep watch on judgements and cruel deeds, givers of wealth; for this royal right also they received;—then they who dwell on Olympus made a second generation which was of silver and less noble by far. It was like the golden race neither in body nor in spirit. A child was brought up at his good mother's side an hundred years, an utter simpleton, playing childishly in his own home. But when they were full grown and were come to the full measure of their prime, they lived only a little time and that in sorrow because of their foolishness, for they could not keep from sinning and from wronging one another, nor would they serve the immortals, nor sacrifice on the holy altars of the blessed ones as it is right for men to do wherever they dwell. Then Zeus the son of Cronos was angry and put them away, because they would not give honour to the blessed gods who live on Olympus.

But when earth had covered this generation also—they are called blessed spirits of the underworld by men, and, though they are of second order, yet honour attends them also—Zeus the Father made a third generation of mortal men, a brazen race, sprung from ash-trees; and it was in no way equal to the silver age, but was terrible and strong. They loved the lamentable works of Ares and deeds of violence; they ate no bread, but were hard of heart like adamant, fearful men. Great was their strength and unconquerable the arms which grew from their shoulders on their strong limbs. Their armour was of bronze, and their houses of bronze, and of bronze were their implements: there was no black iron. These were destroyed by their own hands and passed to the dank house of chill Hades, and left no name: terrible though they were, black Death seized them, and they left the bright light of the sun.

But when earth had covered this generation also, Zeus the son of Cronos made yet another, the fourth, upon the fruitful earth, which was nobler and more righteous, a god-like race of hero-men who are called demi-gods, the race before our own, throughout the boundless earth. Grim war and dread battle destroyed a part of them, some in the land of Cadmus at seven-gated Thebe when they fought for the flocks of Oedipus, and some, when it had brought them in ships over the great sea gulf to Troy for rich-haired Helen's sake: there death's end enshrouded a part of them. But to the others father Zeus the son of Cronos gave a living and an abode apart from men, and made them dwell at the ends of earth. And they live untouched by sorrow in the islands of the blessed along the shore of deep swirling Ocean, happy heroes for whom the grain-giving earth bears honey-sweet fruit flourishing thrice a year, far from the deathless gods, and Cronos rules over them; for the father of men and gods released him from his bonds. And these last equally have honour and glory.

And again far-seeing Zeus made yet another generation, the fifth, of men who are upon the bounteous earth.

Thereafter, would that I were not among the men of the fifth generation, but either had died before or been born afterwards. For now truly is a race of iron, and men never rest from labour and sorrow by day, and from perishing by night; and the gods shall lay sore trouble upon them. But, notwithstanding, even these shall have some good mingled with their evils. And Zeus will destroy this race of mortal men also when they come to have grey hair on the temples at their birth. The father will not agree with his children, nor the children with their father, nor guest with his host, nor comrade with comrade; nor will brother be dear to brother as aforetime. Men will dishonour their parents as they grow quickly old, and will carp at them, chiding them with bitter words, hard-hearted they, not knowing the fear of the gods. They will not repay their aged parents the cost of their nurture, for might shall be their right: and one man will sack another's city. There will be no favour for the man who keeps his oath or for the just or for the good; but rather men will praise the evil-doer and his violent dealing. Strength will be right and reverence will cease to be; and the wicked will hurt the worthy man, speaking false words against him, and will swear an oath upon them. Envy, foul-mouthed, delighting in evil, with scowling face, will go along with wretched men one and all. And then Aidos and Nemesis, with their sweet forms wrapped in white robes, will go from the wide-pathed earth and forsake mankind to join the company of the deathless gods: and bitter sorrows will be left for mortal men, and there will be no help against evil.

And now I will tell a fable for princes who themselves understand. Thus said the hawk to the nightingale with speckled neck, while he carried her high up among the clouds, gripped fast in his talons, and she, pierced by his crooked talons, cried pitifully. To her he spoke disdainfully: "Miserable thing, why do you cry out? One far stronger than you now holds you fast, and you must go wherever I take you, songstress as you are. And if I please I will make my meal of you, or let you go. He is a fool who tries to withstand the stronger, for he does not get the mastery and suffers pain besides his shame." So said the swiftly flying hawk, the long-winged bird.

But you, Perses, listen to right and do not foster violence; for violence is bad for a poor man. Even the prosperous cannot easily bear its burden, but is weighed down under it when he has fallen into delusion. The better path is to go by on the other side towards justice; for Justice beats Outrage when she comes at length to the end of the race. But only when he has suffered does the fool learn this. For Oath keeps pace with wrong judgements. There is a noise when Justice is being dragged in the way where those who devour bribes and give sentence with crooked judgements, take her. And she, wrapped in mist, follows to the city and haunts of the people, weeping, and bringing mischief to men, even to such as have driven her forth in that they did not deal straightly with her.

But they who give straight judgements to strangers and to the men of the land, and go not aside from what is just, their city flourishes, and the people prosper in it: Peace, the nurse of children, is abroad in their land, and all-seeing Zeus never decrees cruel war against them. Neither famine nor disaster ever haunt men who do true justice; but light-heartedly they tend the fields which are all their care. The earth bears them victual in plenty, and on the mountains the oak bears acorns upon the top and bees in the midst. Their woolly sheep are laden with fleeces; their women bear children like their parents. They flourish continually with good things, and do not travel on ships, for the grain-giving earth bears them fruit.

But for those who practise violence and cruel deeds far-seeing Zeus, the son of Cronos, ordains a punishment. Often even a whole city suffers for a bad man who sins and devises presumptuous deeds, and the son of Cronos lays great trouble upon the people, famine and plague together, so that the men perish away, and their women do not bear children, and their houses become few, through the contriving of Olympian Zeus. And again, at another time, the son of Cronos either destroys their wide army, or their walls, or else makes an end of their ships on the sea.

You princes, mark well this punishment you also; for the deathless gods are near among men and mark all those who oppress their fellows with crooked judgements, and reck not the anger of the gods. For upon the bounteous earth Zeus has thrice ten thousand spirits, watchers of mortal men, and these keep watch on judgements and deeds of wrong as they roam, clothed in mist, all over the earth. And there is virgin Justice, the daughter of Zeus, who is honoured and reverenced among the gods who dwell on Olympus, and whenever anyone hurts her with lying slander, she sits beside her father, Zeus the son of Cronos, and tells him of men's wicked heart, until the people pay for the mad folly of their princes who, evilly minded, pervert judgement and give sentence crookedly. Keep watch against this, you princes, and make straight your judgements, you who devour bribes; put crooked judgements altogether from your thoughts.

He does mischief to himself who does mischief to another, and evil planned harms the plotter most.

The eye of Zeus, seeing all and understanding all, beholds these things too, if so he will, and fails not to mark what sort of justice is this that the city keeps within it. Now, therefore, may neither I myself be righteous among men, nor my son—for then it is a bad thing to be righteous—if indeed the unrighteous shall have the greater right. But I think that all-wise Zeus will not yet bring that to pass.

But you, Perses, lay up these things within your heart and listen now to right, ceasing altogether to think of violence. For the son of Cronos has ordained this law for men, that fishes and beasts and winged fowls should devour one another, for right is not in them; but to mankind he gave right which proves far the best.

Part Three

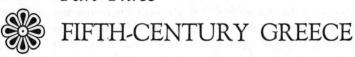 FIFTH-CENTURY GREECE

In the 300 years which separate Homer and Hesiod from the flowering of Athens there was a proliferation and deepening of the Greek genius in literature and in philosophical speculation. These centuries also witnessed political changes and an economic expansion which carried Greek colonists and traders to the far edges of the Mediterranean and of the Black Sea. Feudal-like societies had either retained a now cultured aristocracy or had turned into democracies, enlightened tyrannies, or commercial oligarchies. The Greeks had never united into a national state, but independent or leagued Greek cities flourished not only on the Greek mainland, but also on the coast of Asia Minor, on the Aegean islands, and in Sicily and southern Italy ("Greater Greece"). Each area and period had its literary monuments—personal lyric, lampoon, martial poetry, chorals, political poetry, elegy, philosophical poetry, drama. The age of prose had not yet come, but poetic forms were found to express adequately the still comparatively un-abstract modes of thought. A few poet-thinkers were struggling with problems of human ideals and conduct and their relation to the divine, or (at the end of this period) were seeking to describe the nature and history of the physical universe. One of the most interesting of these is Xenophanes, who attacked the anthropomorphic character and immoral behavior of the gods as pictured in Homer and Hesiod and attacked as well the traditional eminence of the athlete in the scale of Hellenic ideals. He represents, as does apparently the later Heraclitus, the beginnings of a moralistic and intellectualist reaction against the received tradition.

The rise of the city-state (*polis*) as the center of all political and social responsibility had created very special problems in relation to the tradition. Laws and loyalties applicable to a feudal or family-centered society—and often enshrined in religious beliefs—conflicted in many cases with the realities and demands of the new civic life. During the century which began about 500 B.C. solutions were developed at various levels of sophistication to the critical problem of individual conscience in a highly organized *polis*. Although it would be false at any period to think of Greek history and culture in terms of one or two cities— there was continuing independence and rivalry, and a flowering of many cities—the fifth century B.C. is often seen as a polarization in ideals, as in power, between Sparta and Athens. The former had been forced historically into the role of a military state, spare, unintellectual, traditionalist; the latter, dependent on naval power and an expanding economy, was developing an independence of political spirit and magnificence of cultural expression such as has seldom if ever been equalled.

Herodotus: The Defense of Thermopylae

The most important event of the fifth century B.C. for the Greeks was the attack on the Greek mainland by Xerxes, king of the Medes and the Persians. His father, Darius, had dispatched a punitive expedition against the Athenians for the aid they had given rebellious Greek cities in Asia Minor, but that expedition had been repulsed at Marathon, near Athens, in 490 B.C. Ten years later Xerxes determined to reduce these troublesome neighbors and personally led the full strength of his mighty empire against them on land and sea. With only a few defections the Greek cities rallied to oppose him in a show of Hellenic unity unknown since the fabled Trojan expedition. In this conflict Athens in particular and Sparta too gained their titles to the leadership of Greece. It was the strategy of Athens under the inspired leadership of Themistocles which led to the utter defeat of the Persian fleet in the Bay of Salamis, while Xerxes watched from a golden throne what he had expected to be a smashing victory.

Praise of Athens and the Greeks found expression in every form of literature. The victory was interpreted by all as the triumph of free men over the minions of oriental tyranny. The first great European historian, Herodotus, took as his theme the conflict of east and west in its various manifestations since the Trojan war, and in a sweeping account of truly epic proportion told the story down to the Persian defeat. Sparta (whose other name was Lacedaemon) had produced a remarkable ideal of personal military prowess reminiscent of the *Iliad* combined with an absolute devotion to duty and to the state which was the mark of a later age. Herodotus illuminates this ideal and contrasts it with Persian despotism in one of the most vivid sections of his *History*, in which he describes the Spartan defense of the pass of Thermopylae.

The following passages (with omissions) from Herodotus, *History* 8.201-226, are from the translation by George Rawlinson.

King Xerxes pitched his camp in the region of Malis called Trachinia, while on their side the Greeks occupied the straits. These straits the Greeks in general call Thermopylæ (the Hot Gates); but the natives, and those who dwell in the neighbourhood, call them Pylæ (the Gates). Here then the two armies took their stand; the one master of all the region lying north of Trachis, the other of the country extending southward of that place to the verge of the continent.

*   *   *

The various nations had each captains of their own under whom they served; but the one to whom all especially looked up, and who had the command of the entire force, was the Lacedæmonian, Leonidas. He had now come to Thermopylæ, accompanied by the three hundred men which the law assigned him, whom he had himself chosen from among the citizens, and who were all of them fathers with sons living. On his way he had taken the troops from Thebes, whose number I have already mentioned, and who were under the command of Leontiades the son of Eurymachus. The reason why he made a point of taking troops from Thebes, and Thebes only, was, that the Thebans were strongly suspected of being well inclined to the Medes. Leonidas therefore called on them to come with him to the war, wishing to see whether they would comply with his demand, or openly refuse, and disclaim the Greek alliance. They, however, though their wishes leant the other way, nevertheless sent the men.

The force with Leonidas was sent forward by the Spartans in advance of their main body, that the sight of them might encourage the allies to fight, and hinder them from going over to the Medes, as it was likely they might have done had they seen that Sparta was backward. They intended presently, when they had celebrated the Carneian festival, which was what now kept them at home, to leave a garrison in Sparta, and hasten in full force to join the army. The rest of the allies also intended to act similarly; for it happened that the Olympic festival fell exactly at this same period. None of them looked to see the contest at Thermopylæ decided so speedily; wherefore they were content to send forward a mere advanced guard. Such accordingly were the intentions of the allies.

The Greek forces at Thermopylæ, when the Persian army drew near to the entrance of the pass, were seized with fear; and a council was held to consider about a retreat. It was the wish of the Peloponnesians generally that the army should fall back upon the Peloponnese, and there guard the Isthmus. But Leonidas, who saw with what indignation the Phocians and Locrians heard of this plan, gave his voice for remaining where they were, while they sent envoys to the several cities to ask for help, since they were too few to make a stand against an army like that of the Medes.

While this debate was going on, Xerxes sent a mounted spy to observe the Greeks, and note how many there were, and see what they were doing. He had heard, before he came out of Thessaly, that a few men were assembled at this place, and that at their head were certain Lacedæmonians, under Leonidas, a descendant of Hercules. The horseman rode up to the camp, and looked about him, but did not see the whole army; for such as were on the further side of the wall (which had been rebuilt and was now carefully guarded) it was not possible for him to behold; but he observed those on the outside, who were encamped in front of the rampart. It chanced that at this time the Lacedæmonians held the outer guard, and were seen by the spy, some of them engaged in gymnastic exercises, others combing their long hair. At this the spy greatly marvelled, but he counted their number, and when he had taken accurate note of everything, he rode back quietly; for no one pursued after him, nor paid any heed to his visit. So he returned, and told Xerxes all that he had seen.

Upon this, Xerxes, who had no means of surmising the truth—namely, that the Spartans were preparing to do or die manfully—but thought it laughable that they should be engaged in such employments, sent and called to his presence Demaratus the son of Ariston, who still remained with the army. When he appeared, Xerxes told him all that he had heard, and questioned him concerning the news, since he was anxious to understand the meaning of such behaviour on the part of the Spartans. Then Demaratus said:

"I spake to thee, O King! concerning these men long since, when we had but just begun our march upon Greece; thou, however, didst only laugh at my words, when I told thee of all this, which I saw would come to pass. Earnestly do I struggle at all times to speak truth to thee, sire; and now listen to it once more. These men have come to dispute the pass with us; and it is for this that they are now making ready. 'Tis their custom, when they are about to hazard their lives, to adorn their heads with care. Be assured, however, that if thou canst subdue the men who are here and the Lacedæmonians who remain in Sparta, there is no other nation in all the world which will venture to lift a hand in their defence. Thou hast now to deal with the first kingdom and town in Greece, and with the bravest men."

Then Xerxes, to whom what Demaratus said seemed altogether to surpass belief, asked further, "how it was possible for so small an army to contend with his?"

"O King!" Demaratus answered, "let me be treated as a liar, if matters fall not out as I say."

But Xerxes was not persuaded any the more. Four whole days he suffered to go by, expecting that the Greeks would run away. When, however, he found on the fifth that they were not gone, thinking that their firm stand was mere impudence and recklessness, he grew wroth, and sent against them the Medes and Cissians, with orders to take them alive and bring them into his presence. Then the Medes rushed forward and charged the Greeks, but fell in vast numbers: others however took the places of the slain, and would not be beaten off, though they suffered terrible losses. In this way it became clear to all, and especially to the King, that though he had plenty of combatants, he had but very few warriors. The struggle, however, continued during the whole day.

Then the Medes, having met so rough a reception, withdrew from the fight; and their place was taken by the band of Persians under Hydarnes, whom the King called his "Immortals": they, it was thought, would soon finish the business. But when they joined battle with the Greeks, 'twas with no better success than the Median detachment—things went much as before—the two armies fighting in a narrow space, and the barbarians using shorter spears than the Greeks, and having no advantage from their numbers. The Lacedæmonians fought in a way worthy of note, and showed themselves far more skilful in fight than their adversaries, often turning their backs, and making as though they were all flying away, on which the barbarians would rush after them with much noise and shouting, when the Spartans at their approach would wheel round and face their pursuers, in this way destroying vast numbers of the enemy. Some Spartans likewise fell in these encounters, but only a very few. At last the Persians, finding that all their efforts to gain the pass availed nothing, and that, whether they attacked by divisions or in any other way, it was to no purpose, withdrew to their own quarters.

During these assaults, it is said that Xerxes, who was watching the battle, thrice leaped from the throne on which he sat, in terror for his army.

Next day the combat was renewed, but with no better success on the part of the barbarians. The Greeks were so few that the barbarians hoped to find them disabled, by reason of their wounds, from offering any further resistance; and so they once more attacked them. But the Greeks were drawn up in detachments according to their cities, and bore the brunt of the battle in turns,—all except the Phocians, who had been stationed on the mountain to guard the pathway. So, when the Persians found no difference between that day and the preceding, they again retired to their quarters.

Now, as the King was in a great strait, and knew not how he should deal with the emergency, Ephialtes, the son of Eurydemus, a man of Malis, came to him and was admitted to a conference. Stirred by the hope of receiving a rich reward at the King's hands, he had come to tell him of the pathway which led across the mountain to Thermopylæ.

Great was the joy of Xerxes on this occasion; and as he approved highly of the enterprise which Ephialtes undertook to accomplish, he forthwith sent upon the errand Hydarnes, and the Persians under him. The troops left the camp about the time of the lighting of the lamps. The pathway along which they went was first discovered by the Malians of these parts, who soon afterwards led the Thessalians by it to attack the Phocians, at the time when the Phocians fortified the pass with a wall, and so put themselves under covert from danger. And ever since, the path has always been put to an ill use by the Malians.

The Persians took this path, and, crossing the Asopus, continued their march through the whole of the night, having the mountains of Œta on their right hand, and on their left those of Trachis. At dawn of day they found themselves close to the summit. Now the hill was guarded, as I have already said, by a thousand Phocian men-at-arms, who were placed there to defend the pathway, and at the same time to secure their own country. They had been given the guard of the mountain path, while the other Greeks defended the pass below, because they had volunteered for the service, and had pledged themselves to Leonidas to maintain the post.

The ascent of the Persians became known to the Phocians in the following manner: During all the time that they were making their way

up, the Greeks remained unconscious of it, inasmuch as the whole
mountain was covered with groves of oak; but it happened that the air
was very still, and the leaves which the Persians stirred with their feet
made, as it was likely they would, a loud rustling, whereupon the
Phocians jumped up and flew to seize their arms. In a moment the
barbarians came in sight, and, perceiving men arming themselves, were
greatly amazed; for they had fallen in with an enemy when they expected no opposition. Hydarnes, alarmed at the sight, and fearing lest
the Phocians might be Lacedæmonians, inquired of Ephialtes to what
nation those troops belonged. Ephialtes told him the exact truth, whereupon he arrayed his Persians for battle. The Phocians, galled by the
showers of arrows to which they were exposed, and imagining themselves the special object of the Persian attack, fled hastily to the crest
of the mountain, and there made ready to meet death; but while their
mistake continued, the Persians, with Ephialtes and Hydarnes, not
thinking it worth their while to delay on account of Phocians, passed
on and descended the mountain with all possible speed.

The Greeks at Thermopylæ received the first warning of the destruction which the dawn would bring on them from the seer Megistias, who
read their fate in the victims as he was sacrificing. After this deserters
came in, and brought the news that the Persians were marching round
by the hills: it was still night when these men arrived. Last of all, the
scouts came running down from the heights, and brought in the same
accounts, when the day was just beginning to break. Then the Greeks
held a council to consider what they should do, and here opinions were
divided: some were strong against quitting their post, while others
contended to the contrary. So when the council had broken up, part
of the troops departed and went their ways homeward to their several
states; part however resolved to remain, and to stand by Leonidas to
the last.

It is said that Leonidas himself sent away the troops who departed,
because he tendered their safety, but thought it unseemly that either
he or his Spartans should quit the post which they had been especially
sent to guard. For my own part, I incline to think that Leonidas gave
the order, because he perceived the allies to be out of heart and unwilling to encounter the danger to which his own mind was made up.
He therefore commanded them to retreat, but said that he himself
could not draw back with honour; knowing that, if he stayed, glory
awaited him, and that Sparta in that case would not lose her prosperity.
For when the Spartans, at the very beginning of the war, sent to consult

the oracle concerning it, the answer which they received from the Pythoness was, "that either Sparta must be overthrown by the barbarians, or one of her kings must perish." The remembrance of this answer, I think, and the wish to secure the whole glory for the Spartans, caused Leonidas to send the allies away. This is more likely than that they quarrelled with him, and took their departure in such unruly fashion.

So the allies, when Leonidas ordered them to retire, obeyed him and forthwith departed. Only the Thespians and the Thebans remained with the Spartans; and of these the Thebans were kept back by Leonidas as hostages, very much against their will. The Thespians, on the contrary, stayed entirely of their own accord, refusing to retreat, and declaring that they would not forsake Leonidas and his followers. So they abode with the Spartans, and died with them. Their leader was Demophilus, the son of Diadromes.

At sunrise Xerxes made libations, after which he waited until the time when the forum is wont to fill, and then began his advance. Ephialtes had instructed him thus, as the descent of the mountain is much quicker, and the distance much shorter, than the way round the hills, and the ascent. So the barbarians under Xerxes began to draw nigh; and the Greeks under Leonidas, as they now went forth determined to die, advanced much further than on previous days, until they reached the more open portion of the pass. Hitherto they had held their station within the wall, and from this had gone forth to fight at the point where the pass was the narrowest. Now they joined battle beyond the defile, and carried slaughter among the barbarians, who fell in heaps. Behind them the captains of the squadrons, armed with whips, urged their men forward with continual blows. Many were thrust into the sea, and there perished; a still greater number were trampled to death by their own soldiers; no one heeded the dying. For the Greeks, reckless of their own safety and desperate, since they knew that, as the mountain had been crossed, their destruction was nigh at hand, exerted themselves with the most furious valour against the barbarians.

By this time the spears of the greater number were all shivered, and with their swords they hewed down the ranks of the Persians; and here, as they strove, Leonidas fell fighting bravely, together with many other famous Spartans, whose names I have taken care to learn on account of their great worthiness, as indeed I have those of all the three hundred. There fell too at the same time very many famous Persians: among them, two sons of Darius, Abrocomes and Hyperanthes, his children by Phratagune, the daughter of Artanes. Artanes was brother of King

Darius, being a son of Hystaspes, the son of Arsames; and when he gave his daughter to the King, he made him heir likewise of all his substance; for she was his only child.

Thus two brothers of Xerxes here fought and fell. And now there arose a fierce struggle between the Persians and the Lacedæmonians over the body of Leonidas, in which the Greeks four times drove back the enemy, and at last by their great bravery succeeded in bearing off the body. This combat was scarcely ended when the Persians with Ephialtes approached; and the Greeks, informed that they drew nigh, made a change in the manner of their fighting. Drawing back into the narrowest part of the pass, and retreating even behind the cross wall, they posted themselves upon a hillock, where they stood all drawn up together in one close body, except only the Thebans. The hillock whereof I speak is at the entrance of the straits, where the stone lion stands which was set up in honour of Leonidas. Here they defended themselves to the last, such as still had swords using them, and the others resisting with their hands and teeth; till the barbarians, who in part had pulled down the wall and attacked them in front, in part had gone round and now encircled them upon every side, overwhelmed and buried the remnant which was left beneath showers of missile weapons.

Thus nobly did the whole body of Lacedæmonians and Thespians behave; but nevertheless one man is said to have distinguished himself above all the rest, to wit, Dieneces the Spartan. A speech which he made before the Greeks engaged the Medes, remains on record. One of the Trachinians told him, "Such was the number of the barbarians, that when they shot forth their arrows the sun would be darkened by their multitude." Dieneces, not at all frightened at these words, but making light of the Median numbers, answered, "Our Trachinian friend brings us excellent tidings. If the Medes darken the sun, we shall have our fight in the shade."

Pindar: The Eighth Pythian Ode

Herodotus reports that not long after the battle of Thermopylae some Greek deserters were brought before Xerxes, who asked them where the majority of the Greeks were at that point and what they were doing. When they answered that the Greeks were at the

Olympic festival watching athletic contests and horse races, one of the Persians asked what prize was offered. The victor, they replied, was given a crown of wild olive. At this one of the leading Persian nobles blurted out, "Good god, what kind of men have you brought us to fight against? It's not for money they compete, but for the mere achievement of excellence!"

Hard as it is to make him comprehensible in English translation, no account of the Greek spirit would be complete without some example of the poetry of Pindar. In a series of odes written for the noble young victors in the Olympic and other "national" games he caught the flash of brilliance which for a moment illumined their lives and linked them with the heroic past. Connected perhaps by birth and certainly by sympathy with the somewhat old-fashioned aristocracy of his native Thebes, Pindar shows clearly how the traditional ideal of individual heroic excellence survived into this later age. It was kept alive in large part, we can see, by the four great festivals which in various years brought together competitors from all the cities of the Greek world.

The method of Pindar's poetry is complex, and so is its mood. His method is highly allusive: he links the victor or his family or his city with some great mythological event and gives his praise and advice in terms of the myth. He is conscious too of the god in whose honor the games are held and of the circumstances in which his own victory ode will be sung. His mood is often difficult to assess. Elated himself at the Greek successes in the Persian War, he yet had seen the aristocracy of his native city throw in its lot with the invading enemy. Traditionalist and oligarchic in his sympathies, he saw, as he grew older, the masses in the new, pushing democracies gaining the upper hand everywhere about him. Athens in particular had embarked on an expansionist and imperialist policy in the decades after the Persian defeat and had come into open conflict with the very states he most admired, Thebes and the island of Aegina. The watchword of the latter and their allies was "tranquillity," while Athens stood for activism. Thus through the bright world of Pindaric heroism and youth there flicker not only the shadows of age and personal misfortune (which had given an air of pessimism even to parts of the Homeric epics), but also of political change, the feeling that a great era of settled values was being challenged by violent upstarts.

The following poem was written for Aristomenes, son of Xenarces of Aegina and winner of the boys' wrestling match at the Pythian games, held in honor of Apollo at Delphi, in 446 B.C. Two of his uncles had previously been victors in wrestling, one at the Olympian, the other at the Nemean games. He himself had won local contests at Megara, Marathon, and Aegina.

Pindar, *Pythian* 8, is translated by the editor.

Kindly Tranquillity, daughter of Justice, strengthener of cities, who hold in your hands the master-keys of councils and of wars, receive for Aristomenes this tribute due for a Pythian victory. For you know with perfect timeliness the secret of gentleness, both in giving and in taking.

And yet, when someone stirs his heart to pitiless wrath, sternly you confront the might of your enemies; you plunge Insolence into the deep sea. Your power Porphyrion learned when he recklessly challenged you—since that gain alone rewards that one takes from the home of a willing giver—

and his own insolent violence eventually trips up the boaster: Cilician Typhoeus with his hundred heads was ensnared, yes, and the king of the Giants too. By the thunderbolt were they overcome, and by the arrows of Apollo—Apollo, who with kindly heart welcomed Xenarces' son on his return from Cirrha crowned with a leafy chaplet from Parnassus and with a chorus of triumph in Dorian measure.

Surely close by the Graces has fallen the lot of the island Aegina, where the city of Justice holds sway. She knows the famed glory of Aeacus' sons, and has full-grown renown from of old; famous in song she is as the mother of heroes peerless in many a triumphant conquest and in swift tides of battle;

and illustrious too she is for her men. But time would not last me to dedicate to the lyre and the gentle speech of song all the long tale of glory, for fear that satiety might come and vex us. Let rather the business go swiftly forward which touches me now, the debt that is due you, dear lad, the most recent glory, speeding on the wings of my skill.

For in feats of wrestling you follow close on the track of your mother's brothers, bringing no dishonor on Theognetus, victor at Olympia, nor on the sturdy-limbed triumph of Cleitomachus at the Isthmus. And in exalting your father's house of the Midylidae you earn the praise spoken long ago in dark prophecy by Oïcles' son, when he saw the sons of the Seven standing steadfast in battle before seven-gated Thebes,

at the time when the following generation came on a second expedition from Argos. Thus he spoke while they were fighting: "It is by right of birth that there flames forth in them that noble spirit from their fathers. Alcmaeon I clearly see, foremost to mount the walls of Cadmus, brandishing a speckled dragon on his shining shield,

while the hero Adrastus, who before suffered disaster, is destined now for a happier fate. But the fortune of his household shall fare far otherwise; for he alone of the Danaan host, by a destiny sent from the gods, shall gather the bones of his dead son before he shall, with his people unscathed, safely return

to the broad-spaced streets of Abas." So spoke Amphiaraüs. And I too throw my garlands joyfully over Alcmaeon and sprinkle him with the dew of song, for he met me [in a vision], being my neighbor and warder of my property, when I was on my way to the fabled center of the world [Delphi], and himself had a share in his ancestor's prophetic arts.

But you, far-darting god, who are lord of the famed temple which welcomes all in the deep vales of Pytho, there have you granted [to Aristomenes] the greatest gift of all. And before as well, at home, you brought him a coveted prize in the five-fold contest linked with your own and your sister's festival. I pray, lord, that with willing mind

I may keep due measure in view in every task I undertake. Here beside the sweet-voiced triumph-chorus stands Justice. But I pray that never from the fortunes of your house, Xenarces, the gods' abundant care may pass away. For if a man wins glorious victory without great toil, he seems to many to be a wise man among fools

and to be fencing his life around by the powers of good counsel. Yet these things are not in men's hands; but he that gives is a power divine, which sometimes raises up on high and at another time forcefully brings a man low. In Megara you have won pre-eminence already, and in the lonely plain of Marathon; and in the native games of Hera have you, Aristomenes, been victor in three contests;

and with intent to harm you threw yourself on the bodies of four youths, for whom fate at the Pythian festival had not ordained, as for you, any happy homecoming: not for them, as they returned to their mothers, did sweet laughter awake delight; but they slunk home by a sidepath, shrinking from the taunts of foes, heart-broken by their defeat.

But he who has won some fair new thing flies lightly in his prosperity with high hopes on the wings of his exploits, his mind on things far higher than the thought of gain. Brief is the time in which the happiness of mortal men is in blossom, and even so it falls to the earth again, shattered by some adverse fate.

Creatures of the day, what thing is man? what is he not? Man is but a shadow's dream—But when some heaven-borne brightness comes, men are crowned with radiant light and a gentle life. O beloved Mother, Aegina, pilot this city on the ways of freedom, with the help of Zeus and of mighty Aeacus, and of Peleus and goodly Telamon and Achilles!

Sophocles: The *Antigone*

This was the golden age of Athens. At the very moment when Pindar was writing his eighth Pythian ode in praise of tranquil Aegina, this busy neighboring democracy was beginning the sixteen-year construction of the Parthenon with its magnificent sculptures, the greatest creation of the Athenian age. Attracting as it did the most prominent thinkers and teachers of an age of intellectual ferment, who brought new and challenging ideas about man and society, about the gods and the physical universe, the city became a center of intellectual discussion and debate. The philosopher Anaxagoras was tried for impiety because of his view of the nature of the sun and stars. The itinerant teachers called Sophists—some of whom taught merely argument and rhetoric, others more philosophical topics—were all the rage with the brilliant youth, but suspect to the older generation. Their contrast of "conventional" and "natural" morality, justice, and theology appeared corrosive of established values.

In no other writings of the period were these new issues so subtly combined with a traditional style and manner as in the tragedies of Sophocles. No one else grasped and reproduced so surely the heroic ideal as conceived in the Homeric figure of Achilles, and yet in his plays the issues of right and wrong, of state and individual, of fate and free will, of truth and falsehood are dealt with in the terms of contemporary politics and expanding intellectual horizons.

When the *Antigone* opens, the two sons of Oedipus, who had been cursed by their father after his discovery of his incest, lie dead by each other's hand at the gate of Thebes. The exiled Polyneices has led an expedition from Argos to seize the city from his brother, Eteocles. With the repulse of the invader and the death of Oedipus' two sons, their maternal uncle, Creon, takes command of the city and issues an order that Polyneices is not to be given burial. For the ancient Greeks the failure at least to scatter on the corpse a handful of earth not only dishonored the body but also prevented proper entrance into the afterlife. Antigone, a daughter of Oedipus, performs this simple rite for her brother in willful disobedience of Creon's edict; her guilt is discovered and she appears before the enraged new king. Stubborn, defiant, unbending, she is in many ways an unsympathetic character in her self-righteous appeal to a law higher than the king's decree. But Sophocles, like Homer, knew that the truly heroic figure—out of tune with conventional values and set singlemindedly on an independent course —seemed harsh or even repellent to the average man. Her perseverance in her resolve leads in the play to her sentencing and eventual suicide, but only after her cause has been divinely justified through the blind seer Tiresias, and after Creon's misguided tyranny has been punished by the deaths of his son and wife.

The chorus of Theban elders represents here the pious but limited morality of good, patriotic citizens. Their magnificent ode on the marvels of man—a paean for the confident new intellectual humanism—ends with a warning that the disobedient citizen must, however, be shunned. Little do they realize that Antigone, whose entrance under arrest shocks them as the ode ends, will represent in her very disobedience to man-made rules of the state a marvel surpassing all the rest.

The following passage, lines 1-525 of the *Antigone,* is from the translation by R. C. Jebb.

ANTIGONE: Ismene, sister, mine own dear sister, knowest thou what ill there is, of all bequeathed by Oedipus, that Zeus fulfils not for us twain while we live? Nothing painful is there, nothing fraught with ruin, no shame, no dishonour, that I have not seen in thy woes and mine.

And now what new edict is this of which they tell, that our Captain hath just published to all Thebes? Knowest thou aught? Hast thou heard? Or is it hidden from thee that our friends are threatened with the doom of our foes?

ISMENE: No word of friends, Antigone, gladsome or painful, hath come to me, since we two sisters were bereft of brothers twain, killed in one day by a twofold blow; and since in this last night the Argive host hath fled, I know no more, whether my fortune be brighter, or more grievous.

AN. I knew it well, and therefore sought to bring thee beyond the gates of the court, that thou mightest hear alone.

IS. What is it? 'Tis plain that thou art brooding on some dark tidings.

AN. What, hath not Creon destined our brothers, the one to honoured burial, the other to unburied shame? Eteocles, they say, with due observance of right and custom, he hath laid in the earth, for his honour among the dead below. But the hapless corpse of Polyneices—as rumour saith, it hath been published to the town that none shall entomb him or mourn, but leave unwept, unsepulchred, a welcome store for the birds, as they espy him, to feast on at will.

Such, 'tis said, is the edict that the good Creon hath set forth for thee and for me—yes, for *me*—and is coming hither to proclaim it clearly to those who know it not; nor counts the matter light, but, whoso disobeys in aught, his doom is death by stoning before all the folk. Thou knowest it now; and thou wilt soon show whether thou art nobly bred, or the base daughter of a noble line.

Is. Poor sister—and if things stand thus, what could I help to do or undo?

An. Consider if thou wilt share the toil and the deed.

Is. In what venture? What can be thy meaning?

An. Wilt thou aid this hand to lift the dead?

Is. Thou wouldst bury him, when 'tis forbidden to Thebes?

An. I will do my part—and thine, if thou wilt not—to a brother. False to him will I never be found.

Is. Ah, over-bold! when Creon hath forbidden?

An. Nay, he hath no right to keep me from mine own.

Is. Ah me! think, sister, how our father perished, amid hate and scorn, when sins bared by his own search had moved him to strike both eyes with self-blinding hand; then the mother wife, two names in one, with twisted noose did despite unto her life; and last, our two brothers in one day—each shedding, hapless one, a kinsman's blood—wrought out with mutual hands their common doom. And now *we* in turn—we two left all alone—think how we shall perish, more miserably than all the rest, if, in defiance of the law, we brave a king's decree or his powers. Nay, we must remember, first, that we were born women, as who should not strive with men; next, that we are ruled of the stronger, so that we must obey in these things, and in things yet sorer. I, therefore, asking the Spirits Infernal to pardon, seeing that force is put on me herein, will hearken to our rulers; for 'tis witless to be over busy.

An. I will not urge thee—no, nor, if thou yet shouldst have the mind, wouldst thou be welcome as a worker with *me*. Nay, be what thou wilt; but I will bury him: well for me to die in doing that. I shall rest, a loved one with him whom I have loved, sinless in my crime; for I owe a longer allegiance to the dead than to the living: in that world I shall abide for ever. But if *thou* wilt, be guilty of dishonouring laws which the gods have stablished in honour.

Is. I do them no dishonour; but to defy the State,—I have no strength for that.

An. Such be thy plea—I, then, will go to heap the earth above the brother whom I love.

Is. Alas, unhappy one! How I fear for thee!

An. Fear not for me: guide thine own fate aright.

Is. At least, then, disclose this plan to none, but hide it closely—and so, too, will I.

An. Oh, denounce it! Thou wilt be far more hateful for thy silence, if thou proclaim not these things to all.

Is. Thou hast a hot heart for chilling deeds.

An. I know that I please where I am most bound to please.

Is. Aye, if thou canst; but thou wouldst what thou canst not.

An. Why, then, when my strength fails, I shall have done.

Is. A hopeless quest should not be made at all.

An. If thus thou speakest, thou wilt have hatred from me, and wilt justly be subject to the lasting hatred of the dead. But leave me, and the folly that is mine alone, to suffer this dread thing; for I shall not suffer aught so dreadful as an ignoble death.

Is. Go, then, if thou must; and of this be sure—that, though thine errand is foolish, to thy dear ones thou art truly dear. [*exeunt*]

CHORUS: Beam of the sun, fairest light that ever dawned on Thebè of the seven gates, thou hast shone forth at last, eye of golden day, arisen above Dirce's streams! The warrior of the white shield, who came from Argos in his panoply, hath been stirred by thee to headlong flight, in swifter career; who set forth against our land by reason of the vexed claims of Polyneices; and, like shrill-screaming eagle, he flew over into our land, in snow-white pinion sheathed, with an armèd throng, and with plumage of helms.

He paused above our dwellings; he ravened around our sevenfold portals with spears athirst for blood; but he went hence, or ever his jaws were glutted with our gore, or the Fire-god's pine-fed flame had seized our crown of towers. So fierce was the noise of battle raised behind him, a thing too hard for him to conquer, as he wrestled with his dragon foe.

For Zeus utterly abhors the boasts of a proud tongue; and when he beheld them coming on in a great stream, in the haughty pride of clanging gold, he smote with brandished fire one who was now hasting to shout victory at his goal upon our ramparts.

Swung down, he fell on the earth with a crash, torch in hand, he who so lately, in the frenzy of the mad onset, was raging against us with the blasts of his tempestuous hate. But those threats fared not as he hoped; and to other foes the mighty War-god dispensed their several dooms, dealing havoc around, a mighty helper at our need.

For seven captains at seven gates, matched against seven, left the tribute of their panoplies to Zeus who turns the battle; save those two of cruel fate, who, born of one sire and one mother, set against each other their twain conquering spears, and are sharers in a common death.

But since Victory of glorious name hath come to us, with joy responsive to the joy of Thebè whose chariots are many, let us enjoy forgetfulness after the late wars, and visit all the temples of the gods with night-long dance and song; and may Bacchus be our leader, whose dancing shakes the land of Thebè.

But lo, the king of the land comes yonder, Creon, son of Menoeceus, our new ruler by the new fortunes that the gods have given; what counsel is he pondering, that he hath proposed this special conference of elders, summoned by his general mandate?

CREON: Sirs, the vessel of our State, after being tossed on wild waves, hath once more been safely steadied by the gods: and ye, out of all the folk, have been called apart by my summons, because I knew, first of all, how true and constant was your reverence for the royal power of Laïus; how, again, when Oedipus was ruler of our land, and when he had perished, your steadfast loyalty still upheld their children. Since, then, his sons have fallen in one day by a twofold doom—each smitten by the other, each stained with a brother's blood—I now possess the throne and all its powers, by nearness of kinship to the dead.

No man can be fully known, in soul and spirit and mind, until he hath been seen versed in rule and lawgiving. For if any, being supreme guide of the State, cleaves not to the best counsels, but, through some fear, keeps his lips locked, I hold, and have ever held, him most base; and if any makes a friend of more account than his fatherland, that man hath no place in my regard. For I—be Zeus my witness, who sees all things always—would not be silent if I saw ruin, instead of safety, coming to the citizens; nor would I ever deem the country's foe a friend to myself; remembering this, that our country is the ship that bears us safe, and that only while she prospers in our voyage can we make true friends.

Such are the rules by which I guard this city's greatness. And in accord with them is the edict which I have now published to the folk touching the sons of Oedipus—that Eteocles, who hath fallen fighting for our city, in all renown of arms, shall be entombed, and crowned with every rite that follows the noblest dead to their rest. But for his brother, Polyneices—who came back from exile, and sought to consume utterly with fire the city of his fathers and the shrines of his father's gods—sought to taste of kindred blood, and to lead the remnant into slavery—touching this man, it hath been proclaimed to our people that none shall grace him with sepulture or lament, but leave him unburied, a corpse for birds and dogs to eat, a ghastly sight of shame.

Such the spirit of my dealing; and never, by deed of mine, shall the wicked stand in honour before the just; but whoso hath good will to Thebes, he shall be honoured of me, in his life and in his death.

CH. Such is thy pleasure, Creon, son of Menoeceus, touching this city's foe, and its friend; and thou hast power, I ween, to take what order thou wilt, both for the dead, and for all us who live.

CR. See, then, that ye be guardians of the mandate.

CH. Lay the burden of this task on some younger man.

CR. Nay, watchers of the corpse have been found.

CH. What, then, is this further charge that thou wouldst give?

CR. That ye side not with the breakers of these commands.

CH. No man is so foolish that he is enamoured of death.

CR. In sooth, that is the meed; yet lucre hath oft ruined men through their hopes. [*Enter* GUARD.]

GUARD: My liege, I will not say that I come breathless from speed, or that I have plied a nimble foot; for often did my thoughts make me pause, and wheel round in my path, to return. My mind was holding large discourse with me; 'Fool, why goest thou to thy certain doom?' 'Wretch, tarrying again? And if Creon hears this from another, must not thou smart for it?' So debating, I went on my way with lagging steps, and thus a short road was made long. At last, however, it carried the day that I should come hither—to thee; and, though my tale be nought, yet will I tell it; for I come with a good grip on one hope—that I can suffer nothing but what is my fate.

CR. And what is it that disquiets thee thus?

GU. I wish to tell thee first about myself—I did not do the deed—I did not see the doer—it were not right that I should come to any harm.

CR. Thou hast a shrewd eye for thy mark; well dost thou fence thyself round against the blame—clearly thou hast some strange thing to tell.

GU. Aye, truly; dread news makes one pause long.

CR. Then tell it, wilt thou, and so get thee gone?

GU. Well, this is it: The corpse—some one hath just given it burial, and gone away, after sprinkling thirsty dust on the flesh, with such other rites as piety enjoins.

CR. What sayest thou? What living man hath dared this deed?

GU. I know not; no stroke of pickaxe was seen there, no earth thrown up by mattock; the ground was hard and dry, unbroken, without track of wheels; the doer was one who had left no trace. And when the first day-watchman showed it to us, sore wonder fell on all. The dead man was veiled from us; not shut within a tomb, but lightly strewn with dust, as by the hand of one who shunned a curse. And no sign met the eye as though any beast of prey or any dog had come nigh to him, or torn him.

Then evil words flew fast and loud among us, guard accusing guard; and it would e'en have come to blows at last, nor was there any to hinder. Every man was the culprit, and no one was convicted, but all disclaimed knowledge of the deed. And we were ready to take red-hot iron in our hands, to walk through fire, to make oath by the gods that we had not done the deed, that we were not privy to the planning or the doing.

At last, when all our searching was fruitless, one spake, who made us all bend our faces on the earth in fear; for we saw not how we could gainsay him, or escape mischance if we obeyed. His counsel was that this deed must be reported to thee, and not hidden. And this seemed best; and the lot doomed my hapless self to win this prize. So here I stand, as unwelcome as unwilling, well I wot; for no man delights in the bearer of bad news.

CH. O king, my thoughts have long been whispering, can this deed, perchance, be e'en the work of gods?

CR. Cease, ere thy words fill me utterly with wrath, lest thou be found at once an old man and foolish. For thou sayest what is not to be borne, in saying that the gods have care for this corpse. Was it for high reward of trusty service that they sought to hide his nakedness, who came to burn their pillared shrines and sacred treasures, to burn their land, and scatter its laws to the winds? Or dost thou behold the gods honouring the wicked? It cannot be. No! From the first there were certain in the town that muttered against me, chafing at this edict, wagging their heads in secret; and kept not their necks duly under the yoke, like men contented with my sway.

'Tis by them, well I know, that these have been beguiled and bribed to do this deed. Nothing so evil as money ever grew to be current among men. This lays cities low, this drives men from their homes, this trains and warps honest souls till they set themselves to works of shame; this still teaches folk to practise villanies, and to know every godless deed.

But all the men who wrought this thing for hire have made it sure that, soon or late, they shall pay the price. Now, as Zeus still hath my reverence, know this: I tell it thee on my oath, if ye find not the very author of this burial, and produce him before mine eyes, death alone shall not be enough for you, till first, hung up alive, ye have revealed this outrage, that henceforth ye may thieve with better knowledge whence lucre should be won, and learn that it is not well to love gain from every source. For thou wilt find that ill-gotten pelf brings more men to ruin than to weal.

Gu. May I speak? Or shall I just turn and go?

Cr. Knowest thou not that even now thy voice offends?

Gu. Is thy smart in the ears, or in the soul?

Cr. And why wouldst thou define the seat of my pain?

Gu. The doer vexes thy mind, but I, thine ears.

Cr. Ah, thou art a born babbler, 'tis well seen.

Gu. Maybe, but never the doer of this deed.

Cr. Yea, and more—the seller of thy life for silver.

Gu. Alas! 'Tis sad, truly, that he who judges should misjudge.

Cr. Let thy fancy play with 'judgment' as it will—but, if ye show me not the doers of these things, ye shall avow that dastardly gains work sorrows.

[*exit.*]

Gu. Well, may he be found! so 'twere best. But, be he caught or be he not —fortune must settle that—truly thou wilt not see me here again. Saved, even now, beyond hope and thought, I owe the gods great thanks.   [*exit.*]

Chorus: Wonders are many, and none is more wonderful than man; the power that crosses the white sea, driven by the stormy south-wind, making a path under surges that threaten to engulf him; and Earth, the eldest of the gods, the immortal, the unwearied, doth he wear, turning the soil with the offspring of horses, as the ploughs go to and fro from year to year.

And the light-hearted race of birds, and the tribes of savage beasts, and the sea-brood of the deep, he snares in the meshes of his woven toils, he leads captive, man excellent in wit. And he masters by his arts the beast whose lair is in the wilds, who roams the hills; he tames the horse of shaggy mane, he puts the yoke upon its neck, he tames the tireless mountain bull.

And speech, and wind-swift thought, and all the moods that mould a state, hath he taught himself; and how to flee the arrows of the frost, when 'tis hard lodging under the clear sky, and the arrows of the rushing rain; yea, he hath resource for all; without resource he meets nothing that must come: only against Death shall he call for aid in vain; but from baffling maladies he hath devised escapes.

Cunning beyond fancy's dream is the fertile skill which brings him, now to evil, now to good. When he honours the laws of the land, and that justice which he hath sworn by the gods to uphold, proudly stands his city: no city hath he who, for his rashness, dwells with sin. Never may he share my hearth, never think my thoughts, who doth these things!

[*enter the Guard leading in* ANTIGONE.]

What portent from the gods is this? my soul is amazed. I know her—how can I deny that yon maiden is Antigone?

O hapless, and child of hapless sire, of Oedipus! What means this? Thou brought a prisoner—thou, disloyal to the king's laws, and taken in folly?

GUARD: Here she is, the doer of the deed—we caught this girl burying him —but where is Creon?

CH. Lo, he comes forth again from the house, at our need.

CR. What is it? What hath chanced, that makes my coming timely?

GU. O king, against nothing should men pledge their word; for the after-thought belies the first intent. I could have vowed that I should not soon be here again—scared by thy threats, with which I had just been lashed: but, since the joy that surprises and transcends our hopes is like in fulness to no other pleasure—I have come, though 'tis in breach of my sworn oath, bringing this maid; who was taken showing grace to the dead. This time there was no casting of lots; no, this luck hath fallen to me, and to none else. And now, sire, take her thyself, question her, examine her, as thou wilt; but I have a right to free and final quittance of this trouble.

CR. And thy prisoner here—how and whence hast thou taken her?

GU. She was burying the man; thou knowest all.

CR. Dost thou mean what thou sayest? Dost thou speak aright?

GU. I saw her burying the corpse that thou hadst forbidden to bury. Is that plain and clear?

CR. And how was she seen? How taken in the act?

GU. It befell on this wise. When we had come to the place—with those dread menaces of thine upon us—we swept away all the dust that covered the corpse, and bared the dank body well; and then sat us down on the brow of the hill, to windward, heedful that the smell from him should not strike us; every man was wide awake, and kept his neighbour alert with torrents of threats, if any one should be careless of this task.

So went it, until the sun's bright orb stood in mid heaven, and the heat began to burn: and then suddenly a whirlwind lifted from the earth a storm of dust, a trouble in the sky, and filled the plain, marring all the leafage of its woods; and the wide air was choked therewith: we closed our eyes, and bore the plague from the gods.

And when, after a long while, this storm had passed, the maid was seen;

and she cried aloud with the sharp cry of a bird in its bitterness—even as when, within the empty nest, it sees the bed stripped of its nestlings. So she also, when she saw the corpse bare, lifted up a voice of wailing, and called down curses on the doers of that deed. And straightway she brought thirsty dust in her hands; and from a shapely ewer of bronze, held high, with thrice-poured drink-offering she crowned the dead.

We rushed forward when we saw it, and at once closed upon our quarry, who was in no wise dismayed. Then we taxed her with her past and present doings; and she stood not on denial of aught, at once to my joy and to my pain. To have escaped from ills one's self is a great joy; but 'tis painful to bring friends to ill. Howbeit, all such things are of less account to me than mine own safety.

CR. Thou—thou whose face is bent to earth—dost thou avow, or disavow, this deed?

AN. I avow it; I make no denial.

CR. [To Guard.] Thou canst betake thee whither thou wilt, free and clear of a grave charge. [exit Guard.]

[To Antigone.] Now, tell me thou—not in many words, but briefly—knewest thou that an edict had forbidden this?

AN. I knew it: could I help it? It was public.

CR. And thou didst indeed dare to transgress that law?

AN. Yes; for it was not Zeus that had published me that edict; not such are the laws set among men by the Justice who dwells with the gods below; nor deemed I that thy decrees were of such force, that a mortal could override the unwritten and unfailing statutes of heaven. For their life is not of today or yesterday, but from all time, and no man knows when they were first put forth.

Not through dread of any human pride could I answer to the gods for breaking *these*. Die I must—I knew that well (how should I not?)—even without thy edicts. But if I am to die before my time, I count that a gain: for when any one lives, as I do, compassed about with evils, can such an one find aught but gain in death?

So for me to meet this doom is trifling grief; but if I had suffered my mother's son to lie in death an unburied corpse, that would have grieved me; for this, I am not grieved. And if my present deeds are foolish in thy sight, it may be that a foolish judge arraigns my folly.

CH. The maid shows herself passionate child of passionate sire, and knows not how to bend before troubles.

CR. Yet I would have thee know that o'er-stubborn spirits are most often humbled; 'tis the stiffest iron, baked to hardness in the fire, that thou shalt oftenest see snapped and shivered; and I have known horses that show temper brought to order by a little curb; there is no room for pride, when thou art thy neighbour's slave. This girl was already versed in insolence when she transgressed the laws that had been set forth; and, that done, lo, a second insult, to vaunt of this, and exult in her deed.

Now verily I am no man, she is the man, if this victory shall rest with her, and bring no penalty. No! be she sister's child, or nearer to me in blood than any that worships Zeus at the altar of our house, she and her kinsfolk shall not avoid a doom most dire; for indeed I charge that other with a like share in the plotting of this burial.

And summon her, for I saw her e'en now within, raving, and not mistress of her wits. So oft, before the deed, the mind stands self-convicted in its treason, when folks are plotting mischief in the dark. But verily this, too, is hateful: when one who hath been caught in wickedness then seeks to make the crime a glory.

AN. Wouldst thou do more than take and slay me?

CR. No more, indeed; having that, I have all.

AN. Why then dost thou delay? In thy discourse there is nought that pleases me; never may there be! And so my words must needs be unpleasing to thee. And yet, for glory—whence could I have won a nobler, than by giving burial to my own brother? All here would own that they thought it well, were not their lips sealed by fear. But royalty, blest in so much besides, hath the power to do and say what it will.

CR. Thou differest from all these Thebans in that view.

AN. These also share it; but they curb their tongues for thee.

CR. And art thou not ashamed to act apart from them?

AN. No; there is nothing shameful in piety to a brother.

CR. Was it not a brother, too, that died in the opposite cause?

AN. Brother by the same mother and the same sire.

CR. Why, then, dost thou render a grace that is impious in his sight?

AN. The dead man will not say that he so deems it.

CR. Yea, if thou makest him but equal in honour with the wicked.

AN. It was his brother, not his slave, that perished.

CR. Wasting this land; while *he* fell as its champion.

AN. Nevertheless, Hades desires these rites.

CR. But the good desires not a like portion with the evil.

AN. Who knows but this seems blameless in the world below?

CR. A foe is never a friend—not even in death.

AN. 'Tis not my nature to join in hating, but in loving.

CR. Pass, then, to the world of the dead, and, if thou must needs love, love them. While I live, no woman shall rule me.

Part Four

ATHENIAN CRISIS AND REBIRTH

The city of Athens, with its great port of the Piraeus joined to it by walls four miles long, slowly transformed what had started as a league against the Persians into a dependent empire. Her bustling, expansionist democracy not only supported democratic states which would cooperate more easily with her own, but also began to interfere in the internal affairs of other states, supporting democratic factions in times of civil unrest. The oligarchic states, which looked for leadership to Sparta, became increasingly alarmed, and in 431 B.C. pushed the two great opponents into war. Sparta, a land power, had never known defeat nor lost a citizen through surrender. Athens, a sea power, had been well served by a series of democratic leaders from Themistocles to Pericles, who had built up the particular strengths of the city. The so-called Peloponnesian War was destined to last for twenty-seven years and to end in the utter collapse of Athens. The whole of the Greek world, from the Black Sea to Sicily, became involved, and in the final years even the Persian king played an increasingly important part. Our intimate knowledge of the war is due largely to the masterful history of the Athenian, Thucydides, who traced the background of the conflict and the events of the war until his history broke off seven years before its end. In his searching and dramatic analysis one sees the confident beginnings, the disappointments and disasters which afflicted both sides, the increasing demoralization of ideals under stress, the false hopes and misjudgments which at more than one point almost broke Sparta but at last brought defeat to Athens.

From other sources besides Thucydides we can trace the gathering pessimism and hardening of outlook which these decades of privation and struggle brought to Athens. Men of oligarchic sympathies, like the comic poet Aristophanes, had opposed the war from the beginning. As civil unrest stirred, the Sophists and the teachers of rhetoric were blamed for undermining the old values. The tragic poet Euripides wrote plays denouncing war as a defeat for victor and vanquished alike. In the final years and their aftermath first an oligarchical tyranny and then a vengeful democracy gained control of the city. Early in the war Aristophanes had written a play lampooning an Athenian intellectual named Socrates. In the paroxysm of Athenian life following the war what had been fun became deadly serious. Socrates was one of the victims, put to death on a charge of corrupting the minds of the young and introducing new divinities. All that Athenian democracy and the untrammeled intellect of man had stood for seemed to have been washed away.

Athens was not in fact permanently ruined. During the next sixty years she regained independence and even parts of an empire, and in a final moment of glory, impelled by the eloquence of Demosthenes, she rallied her neighbors in a desperate but unsuccessful resistance to Philip of Macedon. Her truest rebirth, however, came in an unexpected quarter. It was as a reaction to the demoralization of Athenian life that Plato formed his philosophy, and it was as a result of his philosophy that Athens and Greece become henceforth the teachers and preceptors of mankind. In Plato the old Greek ideal of the hero appeared once again in a new form, not different essentially from before, but now projected against a background which was to be meaningful forever in European thought. His successor, Aristotle, probably equal in his influence though in certain respects more provincial in his outlook than Plato, completed in his encyclopedic work the Hellenization of western ideals and modes of thought.

Thucydides: Athens, Pericles, and the Plague

Critics have valued different aspects of Thucydides' history of the Peloponnesian War. His dramatic sense, his passion for accuracy, his carefully paced eloquence, his analytic manner—all these qualities can be found in his work. The account in his sixth and seventh books of Athens' magnificent and disastrous expedition against Sicily shows brilliant narrative power. In these varied respects

Thucydides reflected the fifth-century Greek mind, and in his particular admiration for keenness of intellect he was a true son of Athens. His picture of his native city at the beginning of the war and his assessment of Pericles are high points of historical writing. And with masterful intuition for dramatic juxtaposition he placed between these two accounts his lurid description of the plague at Athens and its moral consequences, the first of his several analyses of social disintegration which seem to show the influence of the new Greek science of medicine. With a similarly objective analysis he proceeds to demonstrate that Pericles' strategy and estimates of strength would have brought victory, had he survived and his policy prevailed. Pericles represents for Thucydides the heroic ideal of a fifth-century democratic *polis*. But Pericles himself fell victim to the plague, and that vision of a city where every man was free finds here its last typically Athenian expression.

The following passages, Thucydides, *Histories*, 2.34-54, 59, 65, are in the translation by Richard Crawley.

In the same winter the Athenians gave a funeral at the public cost to those who had first fallen in this war. It was a custom of their ancestors, and the manner of it is as follows. Three days before the ceremony, the bones of the dead are laid out in a tent which has been erected; and their friends bring to their relatives such offerings as they please. In the funeral procession cypress coffins are borne in cars, one for each tribe; the bones of the deceased being placed in the coffin of their tribe. Among these is carried one empty bier decked for the missing, that is, for those whose bodies could not be recovered. Any citizen or stranger who pleases, joins in the procession: and the female relatives are there to wail at the burial. The dead are laid in the public sepulchre in the most beautiful suburb of the city, in which those who fall in war are always buried; with the exception of those slain at Marathon, who for their singular and extraordinary valour were interred on the spot where they fell. After the bodies have been laid in the earth, a man chosen by the state, of approved wisdom and eminent reputation, pronounces over them an appropriate panegyric; after which all retire. Such is the manner of the burying; and throughout the whole of the war, whenever the occasion arose, the established custom was observed. Meanwhile these were the first that had fallen, and Pericles, son of Xanthippus, was chosen to pronounce their eulogium. When the proper time arrived, he advanced from the sepulchre to an elevated platform in order to be heard by as many of the crowd as possible, and spoke as follows:

'Most of my predecessors in this place have commended him who made this speech part of the law, telling us that it is well that it should be delivered at the burial of those who fall in battle. For myself, I should have thought that the worth which had displayed itself in deeds, would be sufficiently rewarded by honours also shown by deeds; such as you now see in this funeral prepared at the people's cost. And I could have wished that the reputations of many brave men were not to be imperilled in the mouth of a single individual, to stand or fall according as he spoke well or ill. For it is hard to speak properly upon a subject where it is even difficult to convince your hearers that you are speaking the truth. On the one hand, the friend who is familiar with every fact of the story, may think that some point has not been set forth with that fulness which he wishes and knows it to deserve; on the other, he who is a stranger to the matter may be led by envy to suspect exaggeration if he hears anything above his own nature. For men can endure to hear others praised only so long as they can severally persuade themselves of their own ability to equal the actions recounted: when this point is passed, envy comes in and with it incredulity. However, since our ancestors have stamped this custom with their approval, it becomes my duty to obey the law and to try to satisfy your several wishes and opinions as best I may.

'I shall begin with our ancestors: it is both just and proper that they should have the honour of the first mention on an occasion like the present. They dwelt in the country without break in the succession from generation to generation, and handed it down free to the present time by their valour. And if our more remote ancestors deserve praise, much more do our own fathers, who added to their inheritance the empire which we now possess, and spared no pains to be able to leave their acquisitions to us of the present generation. Lastly, there are few parts of our dominions that have not been augmented by those of us here, who are still more or less in the vigour of life; while the mother country has been furnished by us with everything that can enable her to depend on her own resources whether for war or for peace. That part of our history which tells of the military achievements which gave us our several possessions, or of the ready valour with which either we or our fathers stemmed the tide of Hellenic or foreign aggression, is a theme too familiar to my hearers for me to dilate on, and I shall therefore pass it by. But what was the road by which we reached our position, what the form of government under which our greatness grew, what the national habits out of which it sprang; these are questions which I may try to solve before I proceed to my panegyric upon these men; since I think this to be a subject upon which on the present occasion a speaker may properly dwell, and to which the whole assemblage, whether citizens or foreigners, may listen with advantage.

'Our constitution does not copy the laws of neighbouring states; we are rather a pattern to others than imitators ourselves. Its administration favours the many instead of the few; this is why it is called a democracy. If we look to the laws, they afford equal justice to all in their private differences; if to social standing, advancement in public life falls to reputation for capacity, class considerations not being allowed to interfere with merit; nor again does poverty bar the way, if a man is able to serve the state, he is not hindered by the obscurity of his condition. The freedom which we enjoy in our government extends also to our ordinary life. There, far from exercising a jealous surveillance over each other, we do not feel called upon to be angry with our neighbour for doing what he likes, or even to indulge in those injurious looks which cannot fail to be offensive, although they inflict no positive penalty. But all this ease in our private relations does not make us lawless as citizens. Against this fear is our chief safeguard, teaching us to obey the magistrates and the laws, particularly such as regard the protection of the injured, whether they are actually on the statute book, or belong to that code which, although unwritten, yet cannot be broken without acknowledged disgrace.

'Further, we provide plenty of means for the mind to refresh itself from business. We celebrate games and sacrifices all the year round, and the elegance of our private establishments forms a daily source of pleasure and helps to banish the spleen; while the magnitude of our city draws the produce of the world into our harbour, so that to the Athenian the fruits of other countries are as familiar a luxury as those of his own.

'If we turn to our military policy, there also we differ from our antagonists. We throw open our city to the world, and never by alien acts exclude foreigners from any opportunity of learning or observing, although the eyes of an enemy may occasionally profit by our liberality; trusting less in system and policy than to the native spirit of our citizens; while in education, where our rivals from their very cradles by a painful discipline seek after manliness, at Athens we live exactly as we please, and yet are just as ready to encounter every legitimate danger. In proof of this it may be noticed that the Lacedæmonians do not invade our country alone, but bring with them all their confederates; while we Athenians advance unsupported into the territory of a neighbour, and fighting upon a foreign soil usually vanquish with ease men who are defending their homes. Our united force was never yet encountered by any enemy, because we have at once to attend to our marine and to despatch our citizens by land upon a hundred different services; so that, wherever they engage with some such fraction of our strength, a success against a detachment is magnified into a victory over the nation, and a defeat into a reverse suffered at the hands of our entire people. And yet if with habits not of labour but of ease, and courage not of art but of nature, we are still willing to encounter danger, we have the double advantage of escaping the experience of hardships in anticipation and of facing them in the hour of need as fearlessly as those who are never free from them.

'Nor are these the only points in which our city is worthy of admiration. We cultivate refinement without extravagance and knowledge without effeminacy; wealth we employ more for use than for show, and place the real disgrace of poverty not in owning to the fact but in declining the struggle against it. Our public men have, besides politics, their private affairs to attend to, and our ordinary citizens, though occupied with the pursuits of industry, are still fair judges of public matters; for, unlike any other nation, regarding him who takes no part in these duties not as unambitious but as useless, we Athenians are able to judge at all events if we cannot originate, and instead of looking on discussion as a stumbling-block in the way of action, we think it an indispensable preliminary to any wise action at all. Again, in our enterprises we present the singular spectacle of daring and deliberation, each carried to its highest point, and both united in the same persons; although usually decision is the fruit of ignorance, hesitation of reflexion. But the palm of courage will surely be adjudged most justly to those, who best know the difference between hardship and pleasure and yet are never tempted to shrink from danger. In generosity we are equally singular, acquiring our friends by conferring not by receiving favours. Yet, of course, the doer of the favour is the firmer friend of the two, in order by continued kindness to keep the recipient in his debt; while the debtor feels less keenly from the very consciousness that the return he makes will be a payment, not a free gift. And it is only the Athenians who, fearless of consequences, confer their benefits not from calculations of expediency, but in the confidence of liberality.

'In short, I say that as a city we are the school of Hellas; while I doubt if the world can produce a man, who where he has only himself to depend upon, is equal to so many emergencies, and graced by so happy a versatility as the Athenian. And that this is no mere boast thrown out for the occasion, but plain matter of fact, the power of the state acquired by these habits proves. For Athens alone of her contemporaries is found when tested to be greater than her reputation, and alone gives no occasion to her assailants to blush at the antagonist by whom they have been worsted, or to her subjects to question her title by merit to rule. Rather, the admiration of the present and succeeding ages will be ours, since we have not left our power without witness, but have shown it by mighty proofs; and far from needing a Homer for our panegyrist, or other of his craft whose verses might charm for the moment only for the impression which they gave to melt at the touch of fact, we have forced every sea and land to be the highway of our daring, and everywhere, whether for evil or for good, have left imperishable monuments behind us. Such is the Athens for which these men, in the assertion of their resolve not to lose her, nobly fought and died; and well may every one of their survivors be ready to suffer in her cause.

'Indeed if I have dwelt at some length upon the character of our country, it has been to show that our stake in the struggle is not the the same as theirs who have no such blessings to lose, and also that the panegyric of the men over whom I am now speaking might be by definite proofs established. That panegyric is now in a great measure complete; for the Athens that I have celebrated is only what the heroism of these and their like have made her, men whose fame, unlike that of most Hellenes, will be found to be only commensurate with their deserts. And if a test of worth be wanted, it is to be found in their closing scene, and this not only in the cases in which it set the final seal upon their merit, but also in those in which it gave the first intimation of their having any. For there is justice in the claim that steadfastness in his country's battles should be as a cloak to cover a man's other imperfections; since the good action has blotted out the bad, and his merit as a citizen more than outweighed his demerits as an individual. But none of these allowed either wealth with its prospect of future enjoyment to unnerve his spirit, or poverty with its hope of a day of freedom and riches to tempt him to shrink from danger. No, holding that vengeance upon their enemies was more to be desired than any personal blessings, and reckoning this to be the most glorious of hazards, they joyfully determined to accept the risk, to make sure of their vengeance and to let their wishes wait; and while committing to hope the uncertainty of final success, in the business before them they thought fit to act boldly and trust in themselves. Thus choosing to die resisting, rather than to live submitting, they fled only from dishonour, but met danger face to face, and after one brief moment, while at the summit of their fortune, escaped, not from their fear, but from their glory.

'So died these men as became Athenians. You, their survivors, must determine to have as unaltering a resolution in the field, though you may pray that it may have a happier issue. And not contented with ideas derived only from words of the advantages which are bound up with the defence of your country, though these would furnish a valuable text to a speaker even before an audience so alive to them as the present, you must yourselves realise the power of Athens, and feed your eyes upon her from day to day, till love of her fills your hearts; and then when all her greatness shall break upon you, you must reflect that it was by courage, sense of duty, and a keen feeling of honour in action that men were enabled to win all this, and that no personal failure in an enterprise could make them consent to deprive their country of their valour, but they laid it at her feet as the most glorious contribution that they could offer. For this offering of their lives made in common by them all they each of them individually received that renown which never grows old, and for a sepulchre, not so much that in which their bones have been deposited, but that noblest of shrines wherein their glory is laid up to be eternally remembered upon every occasion on which deed or story shall fall for its commemoration. For heroes have the whole earth for their tomb; and in lands far from their own, where the column with its epitaph declares it, there is enshrined in every breast a record unwritten with no tablet to preserve it, except that of the heart. These take as your model, and judging happiness to be the fruit of freedom and freedom of valour, never decline the dangers of war. For it is not the miserable that would most justly be unsparing of their lives; these have nothing to hope for: it is rather they to whom continued life may bring reverses as yet unknown, and to whom a fall, if it came, would be most tremendous in its consequences. And surely, to a man of spirit, the degradation of cowardice must be immeasurably more grievous than the unfelt death which strikes him in the midst of his strength and patriotism!

'Comfort, therefore, not condolence, is what I have to offer to the parents of the dead who may be here. Numberless are the chances to which, as they know, the life of man is subject; but fortunate indeed are they who draw for their lot a death so glorious as that which has caused your mourning, and to whom life has been so exactly measured as to terminate in the happiness in which it has been passed. Still I know that this is a hard saying, especially when those are in question of whom you will constantly be reminded by seeing in the homes of others blessings of which once you also boasted: for grief is felt not so much for the want of what we have never known, as for the loss of that to which we have been long accustomed. Yet you who are still of an age to beget children must bear up in the hope of having others in their stead; not only will they help you to forget those whom you have lost, but will be to the state at once a reinforcement and a security; for never can a fair or just policy be expected of the citizen who does not, like his fellows, bring to the decision the interests and apprehensions of a father. While those of you who have passed your prime must congratulate yourselves with the thought that the best part of your life was fortunate, and that the brief span that remains will be cheered by the fame of the departed. For it is only the love of honour that never grows old; and honour it is, not gain, as some would have it, that rejoices the heart of age and helplessness.

'Turning to the sons or brothers of the dead, I see an arduous struggle before you. When a man is gone, all are wont to praise him, and should your merit be ever so transcendent, you will still find it difficult not merely to overtake, but even to approach their renown. The living have envy to contend with, while those who are no longer in our path are honoured with a goodwill into which rivalry does not enter. On the other hand, if I must say anything on the subject of female excellence to those of you who will now be in widowhood, it will be all comprised in this brief exhortation. Great will be your glory in not falling short of your natural character; and greatest will be hers who is least talked of among the men whether for good or for bad.

'My task is now finished. I have performed it to the best of my ability, and in words, at least, the requirements of the law are now satisfied. If deeds be in question, those who are here interred have received part of their honours already, and for the rest, their children will be brought up till manhood at the public expense: the state thus offers a valuable prize, as the garland of victory in this race of valour, for the reward both of those who have fallen and their survivors. And where the rewards for merit are greatest, there are found the best citizens.

'And now that you have brought to a close your lamentations for your relatives, you may depart.'

Such was the funeral that took place during this winter, with which the first year of the war came to an end. In the first days of summer the Lacedæmonians and their allies, with two-thirds of their forces as before, invaded Attica, under the command of Archidamus, son of Zeuxidamus, king of Lacedæmon, and sat down and laid waste the country. Not many days after their arrival in Attica the plague first began to show itself among the Athenians. It was said that it had broken out in many places previously in the neighbourhood of Lemnos and elsewhere; but a pestilence of such extent and mortality was nowhere remembered. Neither were the physicians at first of any service, ignorant as they were of the proper way to treat it, but they died themselves the most thickly, as they visited the sick most often; nor did any human art succeed any better. Supplications in the temples, divinations, and so forth were found equally futile, till the overwhelming nature of the disaster at last put a stop to them altogether.

It first began, it is said, in the parts of Ethiopia above Egypt, and thence descended into Egypt and Libya and into most of the king's country. Suddenly falling upon Athens, it first attacked the population in Piræus—which was the occasion of their saying that the Peloponnesians had poisoned the reservoirs, there being as yet no wells there— and afterwards appeared in the upper city, when the deaths became much more frequent. All speculation as to its origin and its causes, if causes can be found adequate to produce so great a disturbance, I leave to other writers, whether lay or professional; for myself, I shall simply set down its nature, and explain the symptoms by which perhaps it may be recognised by the student, if it should ever break out again. This I can the better do, as I had the disease myself, and watched its operation in the case of others.

That year then is admitted to have been otherwise unprecedentedly free from sickness; and such few cases as occurred, all determined in this. As a rule, however, there was no ostensible cause; but people in good health were all of a sudden attacked by violent heats in the head, and redness and inflammation in the eyes, the inward parts, such as the throat or tongue, becoming bloody and emitting an unnatural and fetid breath. These symptoms were followed by sneezing and hoarseness, after which the pain soon reached the chest, and produced a hard cough. When it fixed in the stomach, it upset it; and discharges of bile of every kind named by physicians ensued, accompanied by very great distress. In most cases also an ineffectual retching followed, producing violent spasms, which in some cases ceased soon after, in others much later. Externally the body was not very hot to the touch, nor pale in its appearance, but reddish, livid, and breaking out into small pustules and ulcers. But internally it burned so that the patient could not bear to have on him clothing or linen even of the very lightest description; or indeed to be otherwise than stark naked. What they would have liked best would have been to throw themselves into cold water; as indeed was done by some of the neglected sick, who plunged into the rain-tanks in their agonies of unquenchable thirst; though it made no difference whether they drank little or much. Besides this, the miserable feeling of not being able to rest or sleep never ceased to torment them. The body meanwhile did not waste away so long as the distemper was at its height, but held out to a marvel against its ravages; so that when they succumbed, as in most cases, on the seventh or eighth day to the internal inflammation, they had still some strength in them. But if they passed this stage, and the disease descended further into the bowels, inducing a violent ulceration there accompanied by severe diarrhœa, this brought on a weakness which was generally fatal. For the disorder first settled in the head, ran its course from thence through the whole of the body, and even where it did not prove mortal, it still left its mark on the extremities; for it settled in the privy parts, the fingers and the toes, and many escaped with the loss of these, some too with that of their eyes. Others again were seized with an entire loss of memory on their first recovery, and did not know either themselves or their friends.

But while the nature of the distemper was such as to baffle all description, and its attacks almost too grievous for human nature to endure, it was still in the following circumstance that its difference from all ordinary disorders was most clearly shown. All the birds and beasts that prey upon human bodies, either abstained from touching them (though there were many lying unburied), or died after tasting them. In proof of this, it was noticed that birds of this kind actually disappeared; they were not about the bodies, or indeed to be seen at all. But of course the effects which I have mentioned could best be studied in a domestic animal like the dog.

Such then, if we pass over the varieties of particular cases, which were many and peculiar, were the general features of the distemper. Meanwhile the town enjoyed an immunity from all the ordinary disorders; or if any case occurred, it ended in this. Some died in neglect, others in the midst of every attention. No remedy was found that could be used as a specific; for what did good in one case, did harm in another. Strong and weak constitutions proved equally incapable of resistance, all alike being swept away, although dieted with the utmost precaution. By far the most terrible feature in the malady was the dejection which ensued when any one felt himself sickening, for the despair into which they instantly fell took away their power of resistance, and left them a much easier prey to the disorder; besides which, there was the awful spectacle of men dying like sheep, through having caught the infection in nursing each other. This caused the greatest mortality. On the one hand, if they were afraid to visit each other, they perished from neglect; indeed many houses were emptied of their inmates for want of a nurse: on the other, if they ventured to do so, death was the consequence. This was especially the case with such as made any pretensions to goodness: honour made them unsparing of themselves in their attendance in their friends' houses, where even the members of the family were at last worn out by the moans of the dying, and succumbed to the force of the disaster. Yet it was with those who had recovered from the disease that the sick and the dying found most compassion. These knew what it was from experience, and had now no fear for themselves; for the same man was never attacked twice—never at least fatally. And such persons not only received the congratulations of others, but themselves also, in the elation of the moment, half entertained the vain hope that they were for the future safe from any disease whatsoever.

An aggravation of the existing calamity was the influx from the country into the city, and this was especially felt by the new arrivals. As there were no houses to receive them, they had to be lodged at the hot season of the year in stifling cabins, where the mortality raged without restraint. The bodies of dying men lay one upon another, and half-dead creatures reeled about the streets and gathered around all the fountains in their longing for water. The sacred places also in which they had quartered themselves were full of corpses of persons that had died there, just as they were; for as the disaster passed all bounds, men, not knowing what was to become of them, became utterly careless of everything, whether sacred or profane. All the burial rites before in use were entirely upset, and they buried the bodies as best they could. Many from want of the proper appliances, through so many of their friends having died already, had recourse to the most shameless sepulchres: sometimes getting the start of those who had raised a pile, they threw their own dead body upon the stranger's pyre and ignited it; sometimes they tossed the corpse which they were carrying on the top of another that was burning, and so went off.

Nor was this the only form of lawless extravagance which owed its origin to the plague. Men now coolly ventured on what they had formerly done in a corner, and not just as they pleased, seeing the rapid transitions produced by persons in prosperity suddenly dying and those who before had nothing succeeding to their property. So they resolved to spend quickly and enjoy themselves, regarding their lives and riches as alike things of a day. Perseverance in what men called honour was popular with none, it was so uncertain whether they would be spared to attain the object; but it was settled that present enjoyment, and all that contributed to it, was both honourable and useful. Fear of gods or law of man there was none to restrain them. As for the first, they judged it to be just the same whether they worshipped them or not, as they saw all alike perishing; and for the last, no one expected to live to be brought to trial for his offences, but each felt that a far severer sentence had been already passed upon them all and hung ever over their heads, and before this fell it was only reasonable to enjoy life a little.

Such was the nature of the calamity, and heavily did it weigh on the Athenians; death raging within the city and devastation without. Among other things which they remembered in their distress was, very naturally, the following verse which the old men said had long ago been uttered:

A Dorian war shall come and with it death.

So a dispute arose as to whether dearth and not death had not been the word in the verse; but at the present juncture, it was of course decided in favour of the latter; for the people made their recollection fit in with their sufferings. I fancy, however, that if another Dorian war should ever afterwards come upon us, and a dearth should happen to accompany it, the verse will probably be read accordingly. The oracle also which had been given to the Lacedæmonians was now remembered by those who knew of it. When the God was asked whether they should go to war, he answered that if they put their might into it, victory would be theirs, and that he would himself be with them. With this oracle events were supposed to tally. For the plague broke out so soon as the Peloponnesians invaded Attica, and never entering Peloponnese (not at least to an extent worth noticing), committed its worst ravages at Athens, and next to Athens, at the most populous of the other towns. Such was the history of the plague.

After the second invasion of the Peloponnesians a change came over the spirit of the Athenians. Their land had now been twice laid waste; and war and pestilence at once pressed heavy upon them. They began to find fault with Pericles, as the author of the war and the cause of all their misfortunes, and became eager to come to terms with Lacedæmon, and actually sent ambassadors thither, who did not however succeed in their mission. Their despair was now complete and all vented itself upon Pericles. When he saw them exasperated at the present turn of affairs and acting exactly as he had anticipated, he called an assembly, being (it must be remembered) still general, with the double object of restoring confidence and of leading them from these angry feelings to a calmer and more hopeful state of mind. He accordingly came forward and spoke as follows:

*   *   *

Such were the arguments by which Pericles tried to cure the Athenians of their anger against him and to divert their thoughts from their immediate afflictions. As a community he succeeded in convincing them; they not only gave up all idea of sending to Lacedæmon, but applied themselves with increased energy to the war; still as private individuals they could not help smarting under their sufferings, the common people having been deprived of the little that they ever possessed, while the higher orders had lost fine properties with costly establishments and buildings in the country, and, worst of all, had war instead of peace. In fact, the public feeling against him did not subside until he had been fined. Not long afterwards, however, according to the way of the multitude, they again elected him general and committed all their affairs to his hands, having now become less sensitive to their private and domestic afflictions, and understanding that he was the best man of all for the public necessities. For as long as he was at the head of the state during the peace, he pursued a moderate and conservative policy; and in his time its greatness was at its height. When the war broke out, here also he seems to have rightly gauged the power of his country. He outlived its commencement two years and six months, and the correctness of his previsions respecting it became better known by his death. He told them to wait quietly, to pay attention to their marine, to attempt no new conquests, and to expose the city to no hazards during the war, and doing this, promised them a favourable result. What they did was the very contrary, allowing private ambitions and private interests, in matters apparently quite foreign to the war, to lead them into projects unjust both to themselves and to their allies—projects whose success would only conduce to the honour and advantage of private persons, and whose failure entailed certain disaster on the country in the war. The causes of this are not far to seek. Pericles indeed, by his rank, ability, and known integrity, was enabled to exercise an independent control over the multitude—in short, to lead them instead of being led by them; for as he never sought power by improper means, he was never compelled to flatter them, but, on the contrary, enjoyed so high an estimation that he could afford to anger them by contradiction. Whenever he saw them unseasonably and insolently elated, he would with a word reduce them to alarm; on the other hand, if they fell victims to a panic, he could at once restore them to confidence. In short, what was nominally a democracy became in his hands government by the first citizen. With his successors it was different. More on a level with one another, and each grasping at supremacy, they ended by committing even the conduct of state affairs to the whims of the multitude. This, as might have been expected in a great and sovereign state, produced a host of blunders, and amongst them the Silician expedition; though this failed not so much through a miscalculation of the power of those against whom it was sent, as through a fault in the senders in not taking the best measures afterwards to assist those who had gone out, but choosing rather to occupy themselves with private cabals for the leadership of the commons, by which they not only paralysed operations in the field, but also first introduced civil discord at home. Yet after losing most of their fleet besides other forces in Sicily, and with faction already dominant in the city, they could still for three years make head against their original adversaries, joined not only by the Sicilians, but also by their own allies nearly all in revolt, and at last by the king's son, Cyrus, who furnished the funds for the Peloponnesian navy. Nor did they finally succumb till they fell the victims of their own intestine disorders. So superfluously abundant were the resources from which the genius of Pericles foresaw an easy triumph in the war over the unaided forces of the Peloponnesians.

Aristophanes: The *Clouds*

No one would call the *Clouds* Aristophanes' best play, but it is typical of his manner, and it has a special interest for cultural historians. In it is depicted the conservative Athenian reaction to the new intellectualism, both in scientific and in ethical realms. In it is preserved the ridicule which Socrates at his trial blamed in part for the prejudice against him. From Plato's *Symposium* it would appear that Socrates and Aristophanes were friendly acquaintances, and one would expect certain parts of the picture to be accurate. It is clear from Plato, for example, that Socrates had an untiring interest in language, both in its structure and in its meaning. Consciousness of grammar, as well as of logic, was only just beginning at this period. It is hard, however, to reconcile Aristophanes' entire portrait of Socrates with the others which we have, and Plato goes out of his way to deny its validity. So if he is taken here as merely a representative type combining all the latest intellectual interests and speculations, then the whole comedy becomes more believable.

In the play Strepsiades has been ruined financially by his son Phidippides' craze for horse-racing. He takes him to Socrates' "think-tank" next door to learn how to win law suits brought against him by his creditors. The following selections are taken from parts of the comedy in which Socrates most appears.

Aristophanes, *Clouds* 94-698 (with omissions), is reprinted from *The Complete Greek Drama*, edited by Whitney J. Oates and Eugene O'Neill, Jr. (Copyright © 1938 by Random House, Inc., and reprinted by permission).

STREPSIADES: That is the Thoughtery of wise souls. There they prove that we are enclosed on all sides under a vast snuffer, which is the sky. If well paid, these men also teach one how to win law-suits, whether they be just or not.

PHIDIPPIDES: What do they call themselves?

STREPS. I don't know exactly, but they are deep thinkers and most admirable people.

PHIDIP. Bah! the wretches! I know them; you mean those quacks with pale faces, those barefoot fellows, such as that miserable Socrates and Chaerephon?

STREPS. Silence! say nothing foolish! If you desire your father not to die of hunger, join their company and let your horses go.

PHIDIP. No, by Bacchus! even though you gave me the pheasants that Leogoras raises.

STREPS. Oh! my beloved son, I beseech you, go and follow their teachings.

PHIDIP. And what is it I should learn?

STREPS. It seems they have two courses of reasoning, the true and the false, and that, thanks to the false, the worst law-suits can be won. If then you learn this science, which is false, I shall not have to pay an obolus of all the debts I have contracted on your account.

PHIDIP. No, I will not do it. I should no longer dare to look at our gallant horsemen, when I had so ruined my tan.

STREPS. Well then, by Demeter! I will no longer support you, neither you, nor your team, nor your saddle-horse. Go and hang yourself; I turn you out of house and home.

PHIDIP. My uncle Megacles will not leave me without horses; I shall go to him and laugh at your anger. [*exit*]

STREPS. One rebuff shall not dishearten me. With the help of the gods I will enter the Thoughtery and learn myself. [*hesitating*] But at my age, memory has gone and the mind is slow to grasp things. How can all these fine distinctions, these subtleties be learned? Bah! why should I dally thus instead of rapping at the door? Slave, slave!

A DISCIPLE [*within*]. A plague on you! Who are you?

STREPS. Strepsiades, the son of Phido, of the deme of Cicynna.

DISCIPLE [*entering*]. You are nothing but an ignorant and illiterate fellow to let fly at the door with such kicks. You have brought on a miscarriage—of an idea!

STREPS. Pardon me, please; for I live far away from here in the country. But tell me, what was the idea that miscarried?

DISCIPLE. I may not tell it to any but a disciple.

STREPS. Then tell me without fear, for I have come to study among you.

DISCIPLE. Very well then, but reflect, that these are mysteries. Lately, a flea bit Chaerephon on the brow and then from there sprang on to the head of Socrates. Socrates asked Chaerephon, "How many times the length of its legs does a flea jump?"

STREPS. And how ever did he go about measuring it?

DISCIPLE. Oh! it was most ingenious! He melted some wax, seized the flea and dipped its two feet in the wax, which, when cooled, left them shod with true Persian slippers. These he took off and with them measured the distance.

STREPS. Ah! great Zeus! what a brain! what subtlety!

DISCIPLE. I wonder what then would you say, if you knew another of Socrates' contrivances?

STREPS. What is it? Pray tell me.

DISCIPLE. Chaerephon of the deme of Sphettia asked him whether he thought a gnat buzzed through its proboscis or through its anus.

STREPS. And what did he say about the gnat?

DISCIPLE. He said that the gut of the gnat was narrow, and that, in passing through this tiny passage, the air is driven with force towards the breech; then after this slender channel, it encountered the rump, which was distended like a trumpet, and there it resounded sonorously.

STREPS. So the ass of a gnat is a trumpet. Oh! what a splendid asservation! Thrice happy Socrates! It would not be difficult to succeed in a law-suit, knowing so much about a gnat's guts! Open, open this home of knowledge to me quickly! Haste, haste to show me Socrates; I long to become his disciple. But do please open the door. [door opens] Ah! by Heracles! what country are those animals from? And who is this man suspended up in a basket?

DISCIPLE. That's *himself*.

STREPS. Who's himself?

DISCIPLE. Socrates.

STREPS. Socrates! Oh! I pray you, call him right loudly for me.

DISCIPLE. Call him yourself; I have no time to waste. [exit]

STREPS. Socrates! my little Socrates!

SOCRATES. Mortal, what do you want with me?

STREPS. First, what are you doing up there? Tell me, I beseech you.

SOCRATES. I am traversing the air and contemplating the sun.

STREPS. Thus it's not on the solid ground, but from the height of this basket, that you slight the gods, if indeed . . .

SOCRATES. I have to suspend my brain and mingle the subtle essence of my mind with this air, which is of the like nature, in order clearly to penetrate the things of heaven. I should have discovered nothing, had I remained on the ground to consider from below the things that are above; for the earth by its force attracts the sap of the mind to itself. It's just the same as with the water-cress.

STREPS. What? Does the mind attract the sap of the water-cress? Ah! my dear little Socrates, come down to me! I have come to ask you for lessons.

SOCRATES. And for what lessons?

STREPS. I want to learn how to speak. I have borrowed money, and my merciless creditors do not leave me a moment's peace; all my goods are at stake.

SOCRATES. And how was it you did not see that you were getting so much into debt?

STREPS. My ruin has been the madness for horses, a most rapacious evil; but teach me one of your two methods of reasoning, the one whose object is not to repay anything, and, may the gods bear witness, that I am ready to pay any fee you may name.

SOCRATES. By which gods will you swear? To begin with, the gods are not a coin current with us.

STREPS. But what do you swear by then? By the iron money of Byzantium?

SOCRATES. Do you really wish to know the truth of celestial matters?

STREPS. Why, yes, if it's possible.

SOCRATES. . . . and to converse with the clouds, who are our genii?

STREPS. Without a doubt.

SOCRATES. Then be seated on this sacred couch.

STREPS. I am seated.

SOCRATES. Now take this chaplet.

STREPS. Why a chaplet? Alas! Socrates, would you sacrifice me, like Athamas?

SOCRATES. No, these are the rites of initiation.

STREPS. And what is it I am to gain?

SOCRATES. You will become a thorough rattle-pate, a hardened old stager, the fine flour of the talkers . . . But come, keep quiet.

STREPS. By Zeus! That's no lie! Soon I shall be nothing but wheatflour, if you powder me in that fashion.

SOCRATES. Silence, old man, give heed to the prayers. Oh! most mighty king, the boundless air, that keepest the earth suspended in space, thou bright Aether and ye venerable goddesses, the Clouds, who carry in your loins the thunder and the lightning, arise, ye sovereign powers and manifest yourselves in the celestial spheres to the eyes of your sage.

* * *

STREPS. By Zeus! Tell me, Socrates, I pray you, who are these women, whose language is so solemn; can they be demi-goddesses?

SOCRATES. Not at all. They are the Clouds of heaven, great goddesses for the lazy; to them we owe all, thoughts, speeches, trickery, roguery, boasting, lies, sagacity.

STREPS. Ah! that was why, as I listened to them, my mind spread out its wings; it burns to babble about trifles, to maintain worthless arguments, to voice its petty reasons, to contradict, to tease some opponent. But are they not going to show themselves? I should like to see them, were it possible.

CHORUS-LEADER. Hail! veteran of the ancient times, you who burn to instruct yourself in fine language. And you, great high-priest of subtle nonsense, tell us your desire. To you and Prodicus alone of all the hollow orationers of today have we lent an ear—to Prodicus, because of his knowledge and his great wisdom, and to you, because you walk with head erect, a confident look, barefooted, resigned to everything and proud of our protection.

STREPS. Oh! Earth! What august utterances! how sacred! how wondrous!

SOCRATES. That is because these are the only goddesses; all the rest are pure myth.

STREPS. But by the earth! is our father, Zeus, the Olympian, not a god?

SOCRATES. Zeus! what Zeus! Are you mad? There is no Zeus.

STREPS. What are you saying now? Who causes the rain to fall? Answer me that!

SOCRATES. Why, these, and I will prove it. Have you ever seen it raining without clouds? Let Zeus then cause rain with a clear sky and without their presence!

STREPS. By Apollo! that is powerfully argued! For my own part, I always thought it was Zeus pissing into a sieve. But tell me, who is it makes the thunder, which I so much dread?

SOCRATES. These, when they roll one over the other.

STREPS. But how can that be? you most daring among men!

SOCRATES. Being full of water, and forced to move along, they are of necessity precipitated in rain, being fully distended with moisture from the regions where they have been floating; hence they bump each other heavily and burst with a great noise.

STREPS. But is it not Zeus who forces them to move?

SOCRATES. Not at all; it's the aerial Whirlwind.

STREPS. The Whirlwind! ah! I did not know that. So Zeus, it seems, has no existence, and it's the Whirlwind that reigns in his stead? But you have not told me yet what makes the roll of thunder?

SOCRATES. Have you not understood me then? I tell you, that the Clouds, when full of rain, bump against one another, and that, being inordinately swollen out, they burst with a great noise.

STREPS. How can you make me credit that?

SOCRATES. Take yourself as an example. When you have heartily gorged on stew at the Panathenaea, you get throes of stomach-ache and then suddenly your belly resounds with prolonged rumbling.

STREPS. Yes, yes, by Apollo! I suffer, I get colic, then the stew sets to rumbling like thunder and finally bursts forth with a terrific noise. At first, it's but a little gurgling *pappax, pappax!* then it increases, *papapappax!* and when I take my crap, why, it's thunder indeed, *papapappax! pappax! papapappax!!* just like the clouds.

SOCRATES. Well then, reflect what a noise is produced by your belly, which is but small. Shall not the air, which is boundless, produce these mighty claps of thunder?

STREPS. And this is why the names are so much alike: crap and clap. But tell

me this. Whence comes the lightning, the dazzling flame, which at times con-
sumes the man it strikes, at others hardly singes him? Is it not plain, that Zeus
is hurling it at the perjurers?

Socrates. Out upon the fool! the driveller! he still savours of the golden age!
If Zeus strikes at the perjurers, why has he not blasted Simon, Cleonymus and
Theorus? Of a surety, greater perjurers cannot exist. No, he strikes his own
temple, and Sunium, the promontory of Athens, and the towering oaks. Now,
why should he do that? An oak is no perjurer.

Streps. I cannot tell, but it seems to me well argued.

Chorus-Leader. Oh, mortal, you who desire to instruct yourself in our great
wisdom, the Athenians, the Greeks will envy you for your good fortune. Only
you must have the memory and ardour for study, you must know how to stand
the tests, hold your own, go forward without feeling fatigue, caring but little
for food, abstaining from wine, gymnastic exercises and other similar follies, in
fact, you must believe as every man of intellect should, that the greatest of all
blessings is to live and think more clearly than the vulgar herd, to shine in the
contest of words.

Streps. If it be a question of hardiness for labour, of spending whole nights
at work, of living sparingly, of fighting my stomach and only eating chickpease,
rest assured, I am as hard as an anvil.

Socrates. Henceforward, following our example, you will recognize no other
gods but Chaos, the Clouds, and the Tongue, these three alone.

Streps. I would not speak to the others, even if I met them in the street; not
a single sacrifice, not a libation, not a grain of incense for them!

Chorus-Leader. Tell us boldly then what you want of us; you cannot fail
to succeed, if you honour and revere us and if you are resolved to become a
clever man.

Streps. I want to be able to turn bad law-suits to my own advantage and to
slip through the fingers of my creditors.

Chorus-Leader. It shall be as you wish, for your ambitions are modest. Commit yourself fearlessly to our ministers, the sophists.

* * *

Socrates. Come, bring your couch out here.

Streps. But the bugs will not allow me to bring it.

Socrates. Have done with such nonsense! place it there and pay attention.

Streps. Well, here I am.

Socrates. Good! Which science of all those you have never been taught do
you wish to learn first? The measures, the rhythms, or the verses?

Streps. But, wretched man, I do not want to learn all this.

Socrates. Then what *do* you want to know?

Streps. Not that, not that, but the art of false reasoning.

Socrates. But you must first learn other things. Come, what are the male
quadrupeds?

STREPS. Oh! I know the males thoroughly. Do you take me for a fool then? The ram, the buck, the bull, the dog, the pigeon.

SOCRATES. Do you see what you are doing? Is not the female pigeon called the same as the male?

STREPS. How else? Come now!

SOCRATES. How else? With you then it's pigeon and pigeon!

STREPS. That's right, by Posidon! but what names do you want me to give them?

SOCRATES. Term the female pigeonnette and the male pigeon.

STREPS. Pigeonnette! hah! by the Air! That's splendid!

SOCRATES. Now I must teach you to distinguish the masculine proper names from those that are feminine.

STREPS. Ah! I know the female names well.

SOCRATES. Name some then.

STREPS. Lysilla, Philinna, Clitagora, Demetria.

SOCRATES. And what are masculine names?

STREPS. They are countless—Philoxenus, Melesias, Amynias.

SOCRATES. But, wretched man, the last two are not masculine.

STREPS. You do not count them as masculine?

SOCRATES. Not at all. If you met Amynias, how would you hail him?

STREPS. How? Why, I should shout, "Hi, there, Amynia!"

SOCRATES. Do you see? it's a female name that you give him.

STREPS. And is it not rightly done, since he refuses military service? But what use is there in learning what we all know?

SOCRATES. You know nothing about it. Come, lie down there.

STREPS. What for?

SOCRATES. Ponder awhile over matters that interest you.

STREPS. Oh! I pray you, not there! but, if I must lie down and ponder, let me lie on the ground.

SOCRATES. That's out of the question. Come! on the couch!

Plato: Socrates' *Defense*

Socrates has always been an enigmatic figure. He had enormous influence on men of the most varied character and interests, many
of whom wrote memoirs or defenses of him. Yet he was condemned
to death by a 501-man jury and executed. He is best known through
the works of Plato, who was less than 30 when Socrates died in
339 B.C. Plato chose the dialogue form in an attempt to catch the
spirit of Socratic conversations—Socrates left no writings—but it is

hard to know how much in the thought itself is really Socrates and how much is Plato. It has often been assumed that the earliest works represent Socrates most faithfully and the later ones much less so.

The *Apology* (or *Defense*), in which Plato re-created the speeches of Socrates at his trial, has always held a special interest, for it would appear almost certainly to resemble the actual scene, and it sketches those aspects of Socrates' character and interests which are developed in greater detail in the dialogues. Here is his strange combination of practicality and a kind of mysticism, of ironic humor and utter seriousness, of sweeping self-assurance and hatred of pretense; but above all here is a man convinced of a rational meaning in things—in words, in thoughts, in nature, and in human events—and tireless in his search for it. This singleness of purpose in pursuing the right course as he perceived it, even to death, links Socrates with an older heroic tradition. Plato's ability to convey the unattractively stubborn and self-righteous aspects of such a character while yet maintaining the sense of heroism is one of the triumphs of his literary art. There is a new feature, however, which puts the Platonic Socrates on a different plane from the heroes of literature and myth: it is his conviction that what he sought, or the way he sought it, would bring some kind of salvation to men.

Socrates makes more than one speech, since in an Athenian Court if the jury voted for conviction, the prosecution and defense each proposed a penalty, and the jury voted again to decide which one to impose.

The following passages are reprinted (with considerable abridgement) from Benjamin Jowett, *The Dialogues of Plato* (4th ed.), Vol. I, by permission of the Clarendon Press, Oxford.

How you, O Athenians, have been affected by my accusers, I cannot tell; but I know that they almost made me forget who I was— so persuasively did they speak; and yet they have hardly uttered a word of truth. But of the many falsehoods told by them, there was one which quite amazed me;—I mean when they said that you should be upon your guard and not allow yourselves to be deceived by the force of my eloquence. To say this, when they were certain to be detected as soon as I opened my lips and proved myself to be anything but a great speaker, did indeed appear to me most shameless—unless by the force of eloquence they mean the force of truth; for if such is their meaning, I admit that I am eloquent. But in how different a way from theirs! Well, as I was saying, they have scarcely spoken the truth at all; from me you shall hear the whole truth, but not delivered after their manner in a set oration duly ornamented with fine words and phrases. No, by heaven! but I shall use the words and arguments which occur to me at the moment, for I am confident in the justice of my cause: at my time of life I ought not to be appearing before you, O men of Athens, in the character of a boy inventing falsehoods—let no one expect it of me. And I must particularly beg of you to grant me this favour:—If I defend myself in my accustomed manner, and you hear me using the words which many of you have heard me using habitually in the agora, at the tables of the money-changers, and elsewhere, I would ask you not to be surprised, and not to interrupt me on this account. For I am more than seventy years of age, and appearing now for the first time before a court of law, I am quite a stranger to the language of the place; and therefore I would have you regard me as if I were really a stranger, whom you would excuse if he spoke in his native tongue, and after the fashion of his country:—Am I making an unfair request of you? Never mind the manner, which may or may not be good; but think only of the truth of my words, and give heed to that: let the speaker speak truly and the judge decide justly.

And first, I have to reply to the older charges and to my first accusers, and then I will go on to the later ones. For of old I have had many accusers, who have accused me falsely to you during many years; and I am more afraid of them than of Anytus and his associates, who are dangerous, too, in their own way.

I will begin at the beginning, and ask what is the accusation which has given rise to the slander of me, and in fact has encouraged Meletus to prefer this charge against me. Well, what do the slanderers say? They shall be my prosecutors, and this is the information they swear against me: 'Socrates is an evil-doer; a meddler who searches into things under the earth and in heaven, and makes the worse appear the better cause, and teaches the aforesaid practices to others.' Such is the nature of the accusation: it is just what you have yourselves seen in the comedy of Aristophanes, who has introduced a man whom he calls Socrates, swinging about and saying that he walks on air, and talking a deal of nonsense concerning matters of which I do not pretend to know either much or little—not that I mean to speak disparagingly of anyone who is a student of natural philosophy. May Meletus never bring so many charges against me as to make me do that! But the simple truth is, O Athenians, that I have nothing to do with physical speculations.

Here, O men of Athens, I must beg you not to interrupt me, even if I seem to say something extravagant. For the word which I will speak is not mine. I will refer you to a witness who is worthy of credit; that witness shall be the god of Delphi—he will tell you about my wisdom, if I have any, and of what sort it is. You must have known Chaerephon; he was early a friend of mine, and also a friend of yours, for he shared in the recent exile of the people, and returned with you. Well, Chaerephon, as you know, was very impetuous in all his doings, and he went to Delphi and boldly asked the oracle to tell him whether—as I was saying, I must beg you not to interrupt—he actually asked the oracle to tell him whether anyone was wiser than I was, and the Pythian prophetess answered that there was no man wiser. Chaerephon is dead himself; but his brother, who is in court, will confirm the truth of what I am saying.

Why do I mention this? Because I am going to explain to you why I have such an evil name. When I heard the answer, I said to myself, What can the god mean? and what is the interpretation of his riddle? for I know that I have no wisdom, small or great. What then can he mean when he says that I am the wisest of men? And yet he is a god, and cannot lie; that would be against his nature. After long perplexity, I thought of a method of trying the question. I reflected that if I could only find a man wiser than myself, then I might go to the god with a refutation in my hand. I should say to him, 'Here is a man who is wiser than I am; but you said that I was the wisest.' Accordingly I went to one who had the reputation of wisdom, and observed him—his name I need not mention, he was a politician; and in the process of examining him and talking with him, this, men of Athens, was what I found. I could not help thinking that he was not really wise, although he was thought wise by many, and still wiser by himself; and thereupon I tried to explain to him that he thought himself wise, but was not really wise; and the consequence was that he hated me, and his enmity was shared by several who were present and heard me. So I left him, saying to myself as I went away: Well, although I do not suppose that either of us knows anything really worth knowing, I am at least wiser than this fellow—for he knows nothing, and thinks that he knows; I neither know nor think that I know. In this one little point, then, I seem to have the advantage of him. Then I went to another who had still higher pretensions to wisdom, and my conclusion was exactly the same. Whereupon I made another enemy of him, and of many others besides him.

This inquisition has led to my having many enemies of the worst and most dangerous kind, and has given rise also to many imputations, including the name of 'wise'; for my hearers always imagine that I myself possess the wisdom which I find wanting in others. But the truth is, O men of Athens, that God only is wise; and by his answer he intends to show that the wisdom of men is worth little or nothing.

*　　　　　*　　　　　*

I have said enough in my defence against the first class of my accusers; I turn to the second class. They are headed by Meletus, that good man and true lover of his country, as he calls himself. Against these, too, I must try to make a defence:—Let their affidavit be read: it contains something of this kind: it says that Socrates is a doer of evil, inasmuch as he corrupts the youth, and does not receive the gods whom the state receives, but has a new religion of his own. Such is the charge; and now let us examine the particular counts. He says that I am a doer of evil, and corrupt the youth; but I say, O men of Athens, that Meletus is a doer of evil, in that he is playing a solemn farce, recklessly bringing men to trial from a pretended zeal and interest about matters in which he really never had the smallest interest. And the truth of this I will endeavour to prove to you.

Come hither, Meletus, and let me ask a question of you. You attach great importance to the improvement of youth?

Yes, I do.

Tell the judges, then, who is their improver; for you must know, as you take such interest in the subject and have discovered their corrupter, and are citing and accusing me in this court. Speak, then, and tell the judges who is the improver of youth:—Observe, Meletus, that you are silent, and have nothing to say. But is this not rather disgraceful, and a very considerable proof of what I was saying, that you have no interest in the matter? Speak up, friend, and tell us who their improver is.

The laws.

But that, my good sir, is not my question. Can you not name some person—whose first qualification will be that he knows the laws?

The judges, Socrates, who are present in court.

What, do you mean to say, Meletus, that they are able to instruct and improve youth?

Certainly they are.

What, all of them, or some only and not others?

All of them.

Truly, that is good news! There are plenty of improvers, then. And what do you say of the audience—do they improve them?

Yes, they do.

And the senators?

Yes, the senators improve them.

But perhaps the members of the assembly corrupt them?—or do they too improve them?

They improve them.

Then every Athenian improves and elevates them; all with the exception of myself; and I alone am their corrupter? Is that what you affirm?

That is what I stoutly affirm.

I am very unfortunate if you are right. But suppose I ask you a question: Is it the same with horses? Does one man do them harm and all the world good? Is not the exact opposite the truth? One man is able to do them good, or at least very few;—the trainer of horses, that is to say, does them good, but the ordinary man does them harm if he has to do with them? Is not that true, Meletus, of horses, or of any other animals? Most assuredly it is; whether you and Anytus say yes or no. Happy indeed would be the condition of youth if they had one corrupter only, and all the rest of the world were their benefactors. But you, Meletus, have sufficiently shown that you never had a thought about the young: your carelessness is plainly seen in your not caring about the very things which you bring against me.

It will be very clear to you, Athenians, that Meletus has never had any care, great or small, about the matter. But still I should like to know, Meletus, in what I am affirmed to corrupt the young. I suppose you mean, as I infer from your indictment, that I teach them not to acknowledge the gods which the state acknowledges, but some other new divinities or spiritual agencies in their stead. These are the lessons by which I corrupt the youth, as you say.

Yes, that I say emphatically.

Then, by the gods, Meletus, of whom we are speaking, tell me and the court, in somewhat plainer terms, what you mean! for I do not as yet understand whether you affirm that I teach other men to acknowledge some gods, and therefore that I do believe in gods, and am not an entire atheist—this you do not lay to my charge,—but only you say that they are not the same gods which the city recognizes—the charge is that they are different gods. Or, do you mean that I am an atheist simply, and a teacher of atheism?

I mean the latter—that you are a complete atheist.

What an extraordinary statement! Why do you think so, Meletus? Do you mean that I do not believe in the godhead of the sun or moon, like the rest of mankind?

I assure you, judges, that he does not: for he says that the sun is stone, and the moon earth.

Friend Meletus, do you think that you are accusing Anaxagoras? Have you such a low opinion of the judges, that you fancy them so illiterate as not to know that these doctrines are found in the books of Anaxagoras the Clazomenian, which are full of them. And so, forsooth, the youth are said to be taught them by Socrates, when they can be bought in the book-market for one drachma at most; and they might pay their money, and laugh at Socrates if he pretends to father these extraordinary views.

And so, Meletus, you really think that I do not believe in any god?

I swear by Zeus that you verily believe in none at all.

Nobody will believe you, Meletus, and I am pretty sure that you do not believe yourself.

I should like you, O men of Athens, to join me in examining what I conceive to be his inconsistency; and do you, Meletus, answer. And I must remind the audience of my request that they would not make a disturbance if I speak in my accustomed manner:

Did ever man, Meletus, believe in the existence of human things, and not of human beings? . . . I wish, men of Athens, that he would answer, and not be always trying to get up an interruption. Did ever any man believe in horsemanship, and not in horses? or in flute-playing, and not in flute-players? My friend, no man ever did; I answer to you and to the court, as you refuse to answer for yourself. There is no man who ever did. But now please to answer the next question: Can a man believe in the existence of things spiritual and divine, and not in spirits or demigods?

He cannot.

How lucky I am to have extracted that answer, by the assistance of the court! But then you swear in the indictment that I teach and believe in divine or spiritual things (new or old, no matter for that); at any rate, I believe in spiritual things,—so you say and swear in the affidavit; and yet if I believe in them, how can I help believing in spirits or demigods; —must I not? To be sure I must; your silence gives consent.

*   *   *

I have said enough in answer to the charge of Meletus: any elaborate defence is unnecessary. You know well the truth of my statement that I have incurred many violent enmities; and this is what will be my destruction if I am destroyed;—not Meletus, nor yet Anytus, but the envy and detraction of the world, which has been the death of many good men, and will probably be the death of many more; there is no danger of my being the last of them.

Someone will say: And are you not ashamed, Socrates, of a course of life which is likely to bring you to an untimely end? To him I may fairly answer: There you are mistaken: a man who is good for anything ought not to calculate the chance of living or dying; he ought only to consider whether in doing anything he is doing right or wrong—acting the part of a good man or of a bad. Whereas, upon your view, the heroes who fell at Troy were not good for much, and the son of Thetis above all, who altogether despised danger in comparison with disgrace; and when he was so eager to slay Hector, his goddess mother said to him that if he avenged his companion Patroclus, and slew Hector, he would die himself—'Fate,' she said, in these or the like words, 'waits for you next after Hector;' he, receiving this warning, utterly despised danger and death, and instead of fearing them, feared rather to live in dishonour, and not to avenge his friend. 'Let me die forthwith,' he replies, 'and be avenged of my enemy, rather than abide here by the beaked ships, a laughing-stock and a burden of the earth.' Had Achilles any thought of death and danger? For wherever a man's place is, whether the place which he has chosen or that in which he has been placed by a commander, there he ought to remain in the hour of danger, taking no account of death or of anything else in comparison with disgrace. And this, O men of Athens, is a true saying.

Strange, indeed, would be my conduct, O men of Athens, if I who, when I was ordered by the generals whom you chose to command me at Potidaea and Amphipolis and Delium, remained where they placed me, like any other man, facing death—if now, when, as I conceive and imagine, God orders me to fulfil the philosopher's mission of searching into myself and other men, I were to desert my post through fear of death, or any other fear; that would indeed be strange, and I might justly be arraigned in court for denying the existence of the gods, if I disobeyed the oracle because I was afraid of death, fancying that I was wise when I was not wise. For the fear of death is indeed the pretence of wisdom, and not real wisdom, being a pretence of knowing the unknown; and no one knows whether death, of which men are afraid because they apprehend it to be the greatest evil, may not be the greatest good. Is not this ignorance of a disgraceful sort, the ignorance which is the conceit that man knows what he does not know? And in this respect only I believe myself to differ from men in general, and may perhaps claim to be wiser than they are:—that whereas I know but little of the world below, I do not suppose that I know: but I do know that injustice and disobedience to a better, whether God or man, is evil and dishonourable, and I will never fear or avoid a possible good rather than a certain evil. And therefore if you let me go now, and are not convinced by Anytus, who said that since I had been prosecuted I must be put to death; (or if not that I ought never to have been prosecuted at all); and that if I escape now, your sons will all be utterly ruined by practising what I teach—if you say to me, Socrates, this time we will not mind Anytus, and you shall be let off, but upon one condition, that you are not to inquire and speculate in this way any more, and that if you are caught doing so again you shall die;—if this was the condition on which you let me go, I should reply: Men of Athens, I honour and love you; but I shall obey God rather than you, and while I have life and strength I shall never cease from the practice and teaching of philosophy, exhorting any one of you whom I meet and saying to him after my manner: You, my friend—a citizen of the great and mighty and wise city of Athens—are you not ashamed of heaping up the largest amount of money and honour and reputation, and caring so little about wisdom and truth and the greatest improvement of the soul, which you never regard nor heed at all?

*   *   *

I have something more to say, at which you may be inclined to cry out; but I believe that to hear me will be good for you, and therefore I beseech you to restrain yourselves. I would have you know, that if you kill such an one as I am, you will injure yourselves more than you will injure me. Nothing will injure me, not Meletus nor yet Anytus—they cannot, for a bad man is not permitted to injure a better than himself. I do not deny that Anytus may, perhaps, kill him, or drive him into exile, or deprive him of civil rights; and he may imagine, and others may imagine, that he is inflicting a great injury upon him: but there I do not agree. For the evil of doing as he is doing—the evil of seeking unjustly to take the life of another—is greater far.

And now, Athenians, I am not going to argue for my own sake, as you may think, but for yours, that you may not sin against God by condemning me, who am his gift to you. For if you kill me you will not easily find a successor to me, who, if I may use such a ludicrous figure of speech, am a sort of gadfly, given to the state by God; and the state is a great and noble steed who is tardy in his motions owing to his very size, and requires to be stirred into life. I am that gadfly which God has attached to the state, and all day long and in all places am always fastening upon you, arousing and persuading and reproaching you. You will not easily find another like me, and therefore I would advise you to spare me. I dare say that you may feel out of temper (like a person who is suddenly awakened from sleep), and you think that you might easily strike me dead as Anytus advises, and then you would sleep on for the remainder of your lives, unless God in his care of you sent you another gadfly. When I say that I am given to you by God, the proof of my mission is this:— if I had been like other men, I should not have neglected all my own concerns or patiently seen the neglect of them during all these years, and have been doing yours, coming to you individually like a father or elder brother, exhorting you to regard virtue; such conduct, I say, would be unlike human nature. If I gained anything, or if my exhortations were paid, there would be some sense in my doing so; but now, as you see for yourselves, not even the unfailing impudence of my accusers dares to say that I have ever exacted or sought pay of anyone; of that they can produce no witness. And I have a sufficient witness to the truth of what I say—my poverty.

Someone may wonder why I go about in private giving advice and busying myself with the concerns of others, but do not venture to come forward in public and advise the state. I will tell you why. You have heard me speak at sundry times and in divers places of a superhuman oracle or sign which comes to me, and is the divinity which Meletus ridicules in the indictment. This sign, which is a kind of voice, first began to come to me when I was a child; from time to time it forbids me to do something which I am going to do, but never commands anything. This is what deters me from being a politician. And rightly, as I think. For I am certain, O men of Athens, that if I had engaged in politics, I should have perished long ago, and done no good either to you or to myself. And do not be offended at my telling you the truth: for the truth is, that no man who sets himself firmly against you or any other multitude, honestly striving to keep the state from many lawless and unrighteous deeds, will save his life; he who will fight for the right, if he would live even for a brief space, must have a private station and not a public one.

*   *   *

I do believe that there are gods, and in a sense higher than that in which any of my accusers believe in them. And to you and to God I commit my cause, to be determined as is best for you and me.

———————————

There are many reasons why I am not grieved, O men of Athens, at the vote of condemnation. I expected it, and am only surprised that the votes are so nearly equal; for I had thought that the majority against me would have been far larger; but now, had thirty votes gone over to the other side, I should have been acquitted. And I may say, I think, that I have escaped Meletus. I may say more; for without the assistance of Anytus and Lycon, anyone may see that he would not have had a fifth part of the votes, as the law requires, in which case he would have incurred a fine of a thousand drachmas.

And so he proposes death as the penalty. And what shall I propose on my part, O men of Athens? Clearly that which is my due. And what is my due? What ought I to have done to me, or to pay—a man who has never had the wit to keep quiet during his whole life; but has been careless of what the many care for—wealth, and family interests, and military offices, and speaking in the assembly, and magistracies, and plots, and parties. Reflecting that I was really too honest a man to be a politician and live, I did not go where I could do no good to you or to myself; but where I could do privately the greatest good (as I affirm it to be) to everyone of you, thither I went, and sought to persuade every man among you that he must look to himself, and seek virtue and wisdom before he looks to his private interests, and look to the state before he looks to the interests of the state; and that this should be the order which he observes in all his actions. What shall be done to such an one? Doubtless some good thing, O men of Athens, if he has his reward; and the good should be of a kind suitable to him. What would be a reward suitable to a poor man who is your benefactor, and who desires leisure that he may instruct you? There can be no reward so fitting as maintenance in the Prytaneum, O men of Athens, a reward which he deserves far more than the citizen who has won the prize at Olympia in the horse or chariot race, whether the chariots were drawn by two horses or by many. For I am in want, and he has enough; and he only gives you the appearance of happiness, and I give you the reality. And if I am to estimate the penalty fairly, I should say that maintenance in the Prytaneum is the just return.

Perhaps you think that I am braving you in what I am saying now, as in what I said before about the tears and prayers. But this is not so. I speak rather because I am convinced that I never intentionally wronged anyone, although I cannot convince you—the time has been too short; if there were a law at Athens, as there is in other cities, that a capital cause should not be decided in one day, then I believe that I should have convinced you. But I cannot in a moment refute great slanders; and, as I am convinced that I never wronged another, I will assuredly not wrong myself. I will not say of myself that I deserve any evil, nor propose any penalty. Why should I? Because I am afraid of the penalty of death which Meletus proposes? When I do not know whether death is a good or an evil, why should I propose a penalty which would certainly be an evil? Shall I say imprisonment? And why should I live in prison, and be the slave of the magistrates of the year—of the Eleven? Or shall the penalty be a fine, and imprisonment until the fine is paid? There is the same objection. I should have to lie in prison, for money I have none, and cannot pay. And if I say exile (and this may possibly be the penalty which you will affix), I must indeed be blinded by the love of life, if I am so irrational as to expect that when you, who are my own citizens, cannot endure my discourses and arguments, and have found them so grievous and odious that you will have no more of them, others are likely to endure me. No indeed, men of Athens, that is not very likely. And what a life should I lead, at my age, wandering from city to city, ever changing my place of exile, and always being driven out! For I am quite sure that wherever I go, there, as here, the young men will flock to listen to me; and if I drive them away, their elders will drive me out at their request; and if I let them come, their fathers and friends will drive me out for their sakes.

Someone will say: Yes, Socrates, but cannot you hold your tongue, and then you may go into a foreign city, and no one will interfere with you? Now I have great difficulty in making you understand my answer to this. For if I tell you that to do as you say would be a disobedience to the God, and therefore that I cannot hold my tongue, you will not believe that I am serious; and if I say again that daily to discourse about virtue, and of those other things about which you hear me examining myself and others, is the greatest good of man, and that the unexamined life is no life for a human being, you are still less likely to believe me. Yet I say what is true, although a thing of which it is hard for me to persuade you. Also, I have never been accustomed to think that I deserve to suffer any harm. Had I money I might have estimated the offence at what I was able to pay, and not have been much the worse. But I have none, and therefore I must ask you to proportion the fine to my means. Well, perhaps I could afford a mina, and therefore I propose that penalty: Plato, Crito, Critobulus, and Apollodorus, my friends here, bid me say thirty minas, and they will be the sureties. Let thirty minas be the penalty; for which sum they will be ample security to you.

———————————

Not much time will be gained, O Athenians, in return for the evil name which you will get from the detractors of the city, who will say that you killed Socrates, a wise man; for they will call me wise, even although I am not wise, when they want to reproach you. If you had waited a little while, your desire would have been fulfilled in the course of nature. For I am far advanced in years, as you may perceive, and not far from death. I am speaking now not to all of you, but only to those who have condemned me to death. And I have another thing to say to them: You think that I was convicted because I had no words of the sort which would have procured my acquittal—I mean, if I had thought fit to leave nothing undone or unsaid. Not so; the deficiency which led to my conviction was not of words—certainly not. But I had not the boldness nor impudence nor inclination to address you as you would have liked me to do, weeping and wailing and lamenting, and saying and doing many things, such indeed as you have been accustomed to hear from others, but I maintain to be unworthy of myself. I thought at the time that I ought not to do anything common or mean when in danger: nor do I now repent of the style of my defence; I would rather die having spoken after my manner, than speak in your manner and live. For neither in war nor yet at law ought I or any man to use every way of escaping death. Often in battle there can be no doubt that if a man will throw away his arms, and fall on his knees before his pursuers, he may escape death; and in other dangers there are other ways of escaping death, if a man has the hardihood to say and do anything. The difficulty, my friends, is not to avoid death, but to avoid unrighteousness; for that runs faster than death. I am old and move slowly, and the slower runner has overtaken me; my accusers are keen and quick, and the faster runner, who is wickedness, has overtaken them. And now I depart hence condemned by you to suffer the penalty of death,—they too go their ways condemned by the truth to suffer the penalty of villainy and wrong; and I must abide by my award—let them abide by theirs. I suppose that these things may be regarded as fated,—and I think that they are well.

And now, O men who have condemned me, I would fain prophesy to you; for I am about to die, and in the hour of death men are gifted with prophetic power. And I prophesy to you who are my murderers, that immediately after my departure punishment far heavier than you have inflicted on me surely awaits you. Me you have killed because you wanted to escape the accuser, and not to give an account of your lives. But that will not be as you suppose: far otherwise. For I say that there will be more accusers of you than there are now; accusers whom hitherto I have restrained: and as they are younger they will be more severe with you, and you will be more offended at them. If you think that by killing men you will stop all censure of your evil lives, you are mistaken; that is not a way of escape which is either very possible, or honourable; the easiest and the noblest way is not to be disabling others, but to be improving yourselves. This is the prophecy which I utter before my departure to the judges who have condemned me.

Friends, who would have acquitted me, I would like also to talk with you about the thing which has come to pass, while the magistrates are busy, and before I go to the place at which I must die. Stay then a little, for we may as well talk with one another while there is time. You are my friends, and I should like to show you the meaning of this event which has happened to me. O my judges—for you I may truly call judges—I should like to tell you of a wonderful circumstance.

Hitherto the divine faculty of which the internal oracle is the source has constantly been in the habit of opposing me even about trifles, if I was going to make a slip or error in any matter; and now as you see there has come upon me that which may be thought, and is generally believed to be, the last and worst evil. But the oracle made no sign of opposition, either when I was leaving my house in the morning, or when I was on my way to the court, or while I was speaking, at anything which I was going to say; and yet I have often been stopped in the middle of a speech, but now in nothing I either said or did touching the matter in hand has the oracle opposed me. What do I take to be the explanation of this silence? I will tell you. It is an intimation that what has happened to me is a good, and therefore those of us who think that death is an evil must be in error. I have this conclusive proof; the customary sign would surely have opposed me had I been going to evil and not to good.

Let us reflect in another way, and we shall see that there is great reason to hope that death is a good; for one of two things—either death is a state of nothingness and utter unconsciousness, or, as men say, there is a change and migration of the soul from this world to another. Now if you suppose that there is no consciousness, but a sleep like the sleep of him who is undisturbed even by dreams, death will be an unspeakable gain. For if a person were to select the night in which his sleep was undisturbed even by dreams, and were to compare with this the other days and nights of his life, and then were to tell us how many days and nights he had passed in the course of his life better and more pleasantly than this one, I think that any man, I will not say a private man, but even the great king will not find many such days or nights, when compared with the others. Now if death be of such a nature, I say that to die is gain; for eternity is then only a single night. But if death is the journey to another place, and there, as men say, all the dead abide, what good, O my friends and judges, can be greater than this? If indeed when the pilgrim arrives in the world below, he is delivered from our earthly professors of justice, and finds the true judges who are said to give judgment there, Minos and Rhadamanthus and Aeacus and Triptolemus, and other sons of God who were righteous in their own life, that pilgrimage will be worth making. What would not a man give if he might converse with Orpheus and Musaeus and Hesiod and Homer? Nay, if this be true, let me die again and again. I myself, too, shall find a wonderful interest in there meeting and conversing with Palamedes, and Ajax the son of Telamon, and any other ancient hero who has suffered death through an unjust judgment; and there will be no small pleasure, as I think, in comparing my own experience with theirs. Above all, I shall then be able to continue my search into true and false knowledge; as in this world, so also in the next; and I shall find out who is wise, and who pretends to be wise, and is not. What would not a man give, O judges, to be able to examine the leader of the great Trojan expedition; or Odysseus or Sisyphus, or numberless others, men and women too! What infinite delight would there be in conversing with them and asking them questions! In another world they do not put a man to death for asking questions: assuredly not. For besides being happier than we are, they will be immortal, if what is said is true.

Wherefore, O judges, be of good cheer about death, and know of a certainty that no evil can happen to a good man, either in life or after death, and that he and his are not neglected by the gods. Nor has my own approaching end happened by mere chance; I see clearly that the time had arrived when it was better for me to die and be released from trouble; therefore the oracle gave no sign, and therefore also I am not angry with my condemners, or with my accusers. But although they have done me no harm, they intended it; and for this I may properly blame them.

Still I have a favour to ask of them. When my sons are grown up, I would ask you, O my friends, to punish them; I would have you trouble them, as I have troubled you, if they seem to care about riches, or anything, more than about virtue; or if they pretend to be something when they are really nothing,—then reprove them, as I have reproved you, for not caring about that for which they ought to care, and thinking that they are something when they are really nothing. And if you do this, I shall have received justice at your hands, and so will my sons.

The hour of departure has arrived, and we go our ways—I to die, and you to live. Which is better God only knows.

Plato: The Simile of the Cave

In his *Phaedo* Plato reproduced the conversation which took place in Socrates' last hours, before he drank the hemlock with that intrepid assurance which had marked his life. Although he had grown up in the demoralization and eventual defeat of the Peloponnesian War, it was the death of Socrates which made Plato turn so strongly against the democratic traditions of his native city. He could never forgive a state, nor approve a form of government, which had brought about that trial and execution. In the *Gorgias* he ridicules the democratic statesmen, Themistocles and Pericles, and denigrates the supposed greatness of Athens in her golden age. In the *Republic* he takes an even more radical step. Here the conversation had begun with an attempted definition of justice in the individual, but after moving from the "just man" to the "just state" (the individual "written large") it had become a discussion of education. Plato was convinced that the whole Greek system and scale of values must be wrong, and nowhere is his conviction clearer than in these passages attacking Homer's and Hesiod's conceptions of gods and heroes, the Athenian tragic drama, contemporary music and dance—in short, the whole traditional content of education. To replace it he develops a new picture of the world and a new type of educated man, the "philosopher-king." In the simile of the cave it becomes clear that he is talking not of mere reform, but rather of a radical "turning of the eye of the soul" to a new vista of existence. The very word corresponds to our (Latin-derived) "conversion," and this is the earliest description of what was destined to become a crucially important and revolutionary concept.

Plato, *Republic* 7:514a-520d, translated by Paul Shorey, is reprinted by permission of the publishers from Loeb Classical Library, *Plato: The Republic,* Vol. II, Cambridge, Mass.: Harvard University Press.

Next, said I, compare our nature in respect of education and its lack to such an experience as this. Picture men dwelling in a sort of subterranean cavern with a long entrance open to the light on its entire width. Conceive them as having their legs and necks fettered from childhood, so that they remain in the same spot, able to look forward only, and prevented by the fetters from turning their heads. Picture further the light from a fire burning higher up and at a distance behind them, and between the fire and the prisoners and above them a road along which a low wall has been built, as the exhibitors of puppet shows have partitions before the men themselves, above which they show the puppets.

All that I see, he said.

See also, then, men carrying past the wall implements of all kinds that rise above the wall, and human images and shapes of animals as well, wrought in stone and wood and every material, some of these bearers presumably speaking and others silent.

A strange image you speak of, he said, and strange prisoners.

Like to us, I said. For, to begin with, tell me do you think that these men would have seen anything of themselves or of one another except the shadows cast from the fire on the wall of the cave that fronted them?

How could they, he said, if they were compelled to hold their heads unmoved through life?

And again, would not the same be true of the objects carried past them?

Surely.

If then they were able to talk to one another, do you not think that they would suppose that in naming the things that they saw they were naming the passing objects?

Necessarily.

And if their prison had an echo from the wall opposite them, when one of the passers-by uttered a sound, do you think that they would suppose anything else than the passing shadow to be the speaker?

By Zeus, I do not, said he.

Then in every way such prisoners would deem reality to be nothing else than the shadows of the artificial objects.

Quite inevitably, he said.

Consider, then, what would be the manner of the release and healing from these bonds and this folly if in the course of nature something of this sort should happen to them. When one was freed from his fetters and compelled to stand up suddenly and turn his head around and walk and to lift up his eyes to the light, and in doing all this felt pain and, because of the dazzle and glitter of the light, was unable to discern the objects whose shadows he formerly saw, what do you suppose would be his answer if someone told him that what he had seen before was all a cheat and an illusion, but that now, being nearer to reality and turned toward more real things, he saw more truly? And if also one should point out to him each of the passing objects and constrain him by questions to say what it is, do you not think that he would be at a loss and that he would regard what he formerly saw as more real than the things now pointed out to him?

Far more real, he said.

And if he were compelled to look at the light itself, would not that pain his eyes, and would he not turn away and flee to those things which he is able to discern and regard them as in very deed more clear and exact than the objects pointed out?

It is so, he said.

And if, said I, someone should drag him thence by force up the ascent which is rough and steep, and not let him go before he had drawn him out into the light of the sun, do you not think that he would find it painful to be so haled along, and would chafe at it, and when he came out into the light, that his eyes would be filled with its beams so that he would not be able to see even one of the things that we call real?

Why, no, not immediately, he said.

Then there would be need of habituation, I take it, to enable him to see the things higher up. And at first he would most easily discern the shadows and, after that, the likenesses or reflections in water of men and other things, and later, the things themselves, and from these he would go on to contemplate the appearances in the heavens and heaven itself, more easily by night, looking at the light of the stars and the moon, than by day the sun and the sun's light.

Of course.

And so, finally, I suppose, he would be able to look upon the sun itself and see its true nature, not by reflections in water or phantasms of it in an alien setting, but in and by itself in its own place.

Necessarily, he said.

And at this point he would infer and conclude that this it is that provides the seasons and the courses of the year and presides over all things in the visible region, and is in some sort the cause of all these things that they had seen.

Obviously, he said, that would be the next step.

Well then, if he recalled to mind his first habitation and what passed for wisdom there, and his fellow bondsmen, do you not think that he would count himself happy in the change and pity them?

He would indeed.

And if there had been honors and commendations among them which they bestowed on one another and prizes for the man who is quickest to make out the shadows as they pass and best able to remember their customary precedences, sequences, and coexistences, and so most successful in guessing at what was to come, do you think he would be very keen about such rewards, and that he would envy and emulate those who were honored by these prisoners and lorded it among them, or that he would feel with Homer and greatly prefer while living on earth to be serf of another, a landless man, and endure anything rather than opine with them and live that life?

Yes, he said, I think that he would choose to endure anything rather than such a life.

And consider this also, said I. If such a one should go down again and take his old place would he not get his eyes full of darkness, thus suddenly coming out of the sunlight?

He would indeed.

Now if he should be required to contend with these perpetual prisoners in 'evaluating' these shadows while his vision was still dim and before his eyes were accustomed to the dark—and this time required for habituation would not be very short—would he not provoke laughter, and would it not be said of him that he had returned from his journey aloft with his eyes ruined and that it was not worth while even to attempt the ascent? And if it were possible to lay hands on and to kill the man who tried to release them and lead them up, would they not kill him?

They certainly would, he said.

This image then, dear Glaucon, we must apply as a whole to all that has been said, likening the region revealed through sight to the habitation of the prison, and the light of the fire in it to the power of the sun. And if you assume that the ascent and the contemplation of the things above is the soul's ascension to the intelligible region, you will not miss my surmise, since that is what you desire to hear. But God knows whether it is true. But, at any rate, my dream as it appears to me is that in the region of the known the last thing to be seen and hardly seen is the idea of good, and that when seen it must needs point us to the conclusion that this is indeed the cause for all things of all that is right and beautiful, giving birth in the visible world to light, and the author of light and itself in the intelligible world being the authentic source of truth and reason, and that anyone who is to act wisely in private or public must have caught sight of this.

I concur, he said, so far as I am able.

Come then, I said, and join me in this further thought, and do not be surprised that those who have attained to this height are not willing to occupy themselves with the affairs of men, but their souls ever feel the upward urge and the yearning for that sojourn above. For this, I take it, is likely if in this point too the likeness of our image holds.

Yes, it is likely.

And again, do you think it at all strange, said I, if a man returning from divine contemplations to the petty miseries of men cuts a sorry figure and appears most ridiculous, if, while still blinking through the gloom, and before he has become sufficiently accustomed to the environing darkness, he is compelled in courtrooms or elsewhere to contend about the shadows of justice or the images that cast the shadows and to wrangle in debate about the notions of these things in the minds of those who have never seen justice itself?

It would be by no means strange, he said.

But a sensible man, I said, would remember that there are two distinct disturbances of the eyes arising from two causes, according as the shift is from light to darkness or from darkness to light, and, believing that the same thing happens to the soul too, whenever he saw a soul perturbed and unable to discern something, he would not laugh unthinkingly, but would observe whether coming from a brighter life its vision was obscured by the unfamiliar darkness, or whether the passage from the deeper dark of ignorance into a more luminous world and the greater brightness had dazzled its vision. And so he would deem the one happy in its experience and way of life and pity the other, and if it pleased him to laugh at it, his laughter would be less laughable than that at the expense of the soul that had come down from the light above.

That is a very fair statement, he said.

Then, if this is true, our view of these matters must be this, that education is not in reality what some people proclaim it to be in their professions. What they aver is that they can put true knowledge into a soul that does not possess it, as if they were inserting vision into blind eyes.

They do indeed, he said.

But our present argument indicates, said I, that the true analogy for this indwelling power in the soul and the instrument whereby each of us apprehends is that of an eye that could not be converted to the light from the darkness except by turning the whole body. Even so this organ of knowledge must be turned around from the world of becoming together with the entire soul, like the scene-shifting periactus in the theater, until the soul is able to endure the contemplation of essence and the brightest region of being. And this, we say, is the good, do we not?

Yes.

Of this very thing, then, I said, there might be an art, an art of the speediest and most effective shifting or conversion of the soul, not an art of producing vision in it, but on the assumption that it possesses vision but does not rightly direct it and does not look where it should, an art of bringing this about.

Yes, that seems likely, he said.

Then the other so-called virtues of the soul do seem akin to those of the body. For it is true that where they do not pre-exist, they are afterward created by habit and practice. But the excellence of thought, it seems, is certainly of a more divine quality, a thing that never loses its potency, but, according to the direction of its conversion, becomes useful and beneficent, or, again, useless and harmful. Have you never observed in those who are popularly spoken of as bad, but smart men how keen is the vision of the little soul, how quick it is to discern the things that interest it, a proof that it is not a poor vision which it has, but one forcibly enlisted in the service of evil, so that the sharper its sight the more mischief it accomplishes?

I certainly have, he said.

Observe then, said I, that this part of such a soul, if it had been hammered from childhood, and had thus been struck free of the leaden weights, so to speak, of our birth and becoming, which attaching themselves to it by food and similar pleasures and gluttonies turn downward the vision of the soul—if, I say, freed from these, it had suffered a conversion toward the things that are real and true, that same faculty of the same men would have been most keen in its vision of the higher things, just as it is for the things toward which it is now turned.

It is likely, he said.

Well, then, said I, is not this also likely and a necessary consequence of what has been said, that neither could men who are uneducated and inexperienced in truth ever adequately preside over a state, nor could those who had been permitted to linger on to the end in the pursuit of culture—the one because they have no single aim and purpose in life to which all their actions, public and private, must be directed, and the others, because they will not voluntarily engage in action, believing that while still living they have been transported to the Islands of the Blessed?

True, he said.

It is the duty of us, the founders, then, said I, to compel the best natures to attain the knowledge which we pronounced the greatest, and to win to the vision of the good, to scale that ascent, and when they have reached the heights and taken an adequate view, we must not allow what is now permitted.

What is that?

That they should linger there, I said, and refuse to go down again among those bondsmen and share their labors and honors, whether they are of less or of greater worth.

Do you mean to say that we must do them this wrong, and compel them to live an inferior life when the better is in their power?

You have again forgotten, my friend, said I, that the law is not concerned with the special happiness of any class in the state, but is trying to produce this condition in the city as a whole, harmonizing and adapting the citizens to one another by persuasion and compulsion, and requiring them to impart to one another any benefit which they are severally able to bestow upon the community, and that it itself creates such men in the state, not that it may allow each to take what course pleases him, but with a view to using them for the binding together of the commonwealth.

True, he said, I did forget it.

Observe, then, Glaucon, said I, that we shall not be wronging, either, the philosophers who arise among us, but that we can justify our action when we constrain them to take charge of the other citizens and be their guardians. For we will say to them that it is natural that men of similar quality who spring up in other cities should not share in the labors there. For they grow up spontaneously from no volition of the government in the several states, and it is justice that the self-grown, indebted to none for its breeding, should not be zealous either to pay to anyone the price of its nurture. But you we have engendered for yourselves and the rest of the city to be, as it were, king bees and leaders in the hive. You have received a better and more complete education than the others, and you are more capable of sharing both ways of life. Down you must go then, each in his turn to the habitation of the others and accustom yourselves to the observation of the obscure things there. For once habituated you will discern them infinitely better than the dwellers there, and you will know what each of the 'idols' is and whereof it is a semblance, because you have seen the reality of the beautiful, the just and the good. So our city will be governed by us and you with waking minds, and not as most cities now which are inhabited and ruled darkly as in a dream by men who fight one another for shadows and wrangle for office as if that were a great good, when the truth is that the city in which those who are to rule are least eager to hold office must needs be best administered and most free from dissension.

Aristotle: "Greatness of Soul"

In protest against the political realities of Athens Plato had turned away to another, ideal world and had founded the first philosophic institute, the Academy, in order to train men in the search for truth.

His most accomplished pupil was Aristotle, a Platonist by training and by philosophic tendency, but with so distinct an individual bent that he founded a new school, the Lyceum, and formed a new system of thought as well. Aristotle conceived of the ideal world not as a separate existence, but as active and mainly identifiable in the world of our experience. For him the realities of life and nature were of prime importance as the key to the ideal. For Plato they had been to a degree illusory. It was thus that Aristotle's school became immersed in historical and scientific research, and it was thus that he, in lecturing on ethics, sketched various real types of men to demonstrate his theory that virtuous qualities were a kind of mean between vices at the two extremes. His view of the world made him less revolutionary than Plato, more accepting of things as he found them. His politics and ethics have for us an element of parochialism in their assumption of the Greek *polis* and Greek standards. But the intellectual force and range of his exposition gave his system a completeness and an authority which for centuries provided in large part the language and the presuppositions of European thought.

In what is perhaps the finest example of Aristotle's frequent summation of Hellenic ideals he comes in his *Ethics* with admiration to the "great-souled man." It is with a shock of unexpected recognition that we find in his precise formulation a picture of the Homeric hero of centuries earlier transformed into contemporary terms. Translation of the word *megalopsychia* has always given scholars difficulty: "greatness of soul" is satisfactorily literal, but what Aristotle is really describing is the classical Greek idea of the heroic.

Aristotle, *Nicomachean Ethics* 4.3 (1123a34-1125a16), trans. Harris Rackham, is reprinted by permission of the publishers from Loeb Classical Library, *Aristotle: Nicomachean Ethics,* Cambridge, Mass.: Harvard University Press.

Greatness of Soul, as the word itself implies, seems to be related to great objects; let us first ascertain what sort of objects these are. It will make no difference whether we examine the quality itself or the person that displays the quality.

Now a person is thought to be great-souled if he claims much and deserves much; he who claims much without deserving it is foolish, but no one of moral excellence is foolish or senseless. The great-souled man is then as we have described. He who deserves little and claims little is modest or temperate, but not great-souled, since to be great-souled involves greatness just as handsomeness involves size: small people may be neat and well-made, but not handsome. He that claims much but does not deserve much is vain; though not everybody who claims more than he deserves is vain. He that claims less than he deserves is small-souled, whether his deserts be great or only moderate, or even though he deserves little, if he claims still less. The most small-souled of all would seem to be the man who claims less than he deserves when his deserts are great, for what would he have done had he not deserved so much?

Though therefore in regard to the greatness of his claim the great-souled man is an extreme, by reason of its rightness he stands at the mean point, for he claims what he deserves; while the vain and the small-souled err by excess and defect respectively.

If then the great-souled man is one who claims and is worthy of much, and the most great-souled is he who claims and is worthy of most, Greatness of Soul must be concerned with some one object especially. 'Worthy' is a term of relation: it denotes having a claim to goods external to oneself. Now the greatest external good we should assume to be the thing which we offer as a tribute to the gods, and which is most coveted by men of high station, and is the prize awarded for the noblest deeds; and such a thing is honour, for honour is clearly the greatest of external goods. Therefore the great-souled man is he who has the right disposition in relation to honours and disgraces. And even without argument it is evident that honour is the object with which the great-souled are concerned, since it is honour above all else which great men claim and deserve.

The small-souled man falls short both as judged by his own deserts and in comparison with the claim of the great-souled man; the vain man on the other hand exceeds as judged by his own standard, but does not however exceed the great-souled man.

And inasmuch as the great-souled man deserves most, he must be the best of men; for the better a man is the more he deserves, and he that is best deserves most. Therefore the truly great-souled man must be a good man. Indeed greatness in each of the virtues would seem to go with greatness of soul. For instance, one cannot imagine the great-souled man running at full speed when retreating in battle, nor acting dishonestly; since what motive for base conduct has a man to whom nothing is [of great importance]? Considering all the virtues in turn, we shall feel it quite ridiculous to picture the great-souled man as other than a good man. Moreover, if he were bad, he would not be worthy of honour, since honour is the prize of virtue, and the tribute that we pay to the good. Greatness of Soul seems therefore to be as it were a crowning ornament of the virtues: it enhances their greatness, and it cannot exist without them. Hence it is hard to be truly great-souled, for greatness of soul is impossible without moral nobility.

Honour and dishonour then are the objects with which the great-souled man is especially concerned. Great honours accorded by persons of worth will afford him pleasure in a moderate degree: he will feel he is receiving only what belongs to him, or even less, for no honour can be adequate to the merits of perfect virtue, yet all the same he will deign to accept their honours, because they have no greater tribute to offer him. Honour rendered by common people and on trivial grounds he will utterly despise, for this is not what he merits. He will also despise dishonour, for no dishonour can justly attach to him. The great-souled man then, as has been said, is especially concerned with honour; but he will also observe due measure in respect to wealth, power, and good and bad fortune in general, as they may befall him; he will not rejoice overmuch in prosperity nor grieve overmuch at adversity. For he does not care much even about honour, which is the greatest of external goods (since power and wealth are desirable only for the honour they bring, at least their possessors wish to be honoured for their sake); he therefore to whom even honour is a small thing will be indifferent to other things as well. Hence great-souled men are thought to be haughty.

But it is thought that the gifts of fortune also conduce to greatness of soul; for the high-born and those who are powerful or wealthy are esteemed worthy of honour, because they are superior to their fellows, and that which is superior in something good is always held in higher honour; so that even these gifts of fortune make men more great-souled, because their possessors are honoured by some people. But in reality only the good man ought to be honoured, although he that has both virtue and fortune is esteemed still more worthy of honour; whereas those who possess the goods of fortune without virtue are not justified in claiming high worth, and cannot correctly be styled great-souled, since true worth and greatness of soul cannot exist without complete virtue. It is true that even those who merely possess the goods of fortune may be haughty and insolent; because without virtue it is not easy to bear good fortune becomingly, and such men, being unable to carry their prosperity, and thinking themselves superior to the rest of mankind, despise other people, although their own conduct is no better than another's. The fact is that they try to imitate the great-souled man without being really like him, and only copy him in what they can, reproducing his contempt for others but not his virtuous conduct. For the great-souled man is justified in despising other people—his estimates are correct; but most proud men have no good ground for their pride.

The great-souled man does not run into danger for trifling reasons, and is not a lover of danger, because there are few things he values; but he will face danger in a great cause, and when so doing will be ready to sacrifice his life, since he holds that life is not worth having at any price.

He is fond of conferring benefits, but ashamed to receive them, because the former is a mark of superiority and the latter of inferiority. He returns a service done to him with interest, since this will put the original benefactor into his debt in turn, and make him the party benefitted. The great-souled are thought to have a good memory for any benefit they have conferred, but a bad memory for those which they have received (since the recipient of a benefit is the inferior of his benefactor, whereas they desire to be superior); and to enjoy being reminded of the former but to dislike being reminded of the latter: this is why the poet makes Thetis not specify her services to Zeus; nor did the Spartans treating with the Athenians recall the occasions when Sparta had aided Athens, but those on which Athens had aided Sparta.

It is also characteristic of the great-souled man never to ask help from others, or only with reluctance, but to render aid willingly; and to be haughty towards men of position and fortune, but courteous towards those of moderate station, because it is difficult and distinguished to be superior to the great, but easy to outdo the lowly, and to adopt a high manner with the former is not ill-bred, but it is vulgar to lord it over humble people: it is like putting forth one's strength against the weak. He will not compete for the common objects of ambition, or go where other people take the first place; and he will be idle and slow to act, except when pursuing some high honour or achievement; and will not engage in many undertakings, but only in such as are important and distinguished. He must be open both in love and in hate, since concealment shows timidity; and care more for the truth than for what people will think; and speak and act openly, since as he despises other men he is outspoken and frank, except when speaking with ironical self-depreciation, as he does to common people. He will be incapable of living at the will of another, unless a friend, since to do so is slavish, and hence flatterers are always servile, and humble people flatterers. He is not prone to admiration, since nothing is [of great importance] to him. He does not bear a grudge, for it is not a mark of greatness of soul to recall things against people, especially the wrongs they have done you; but rather to overlook them. He is no gossip, for he will not talk either about himself or about another, as he neither wants to receive compliments nor to hear other people run down (nor is he lavish of praise either); and so he is not given to speaking evil himself,

even of his enemies, except when he deliberately intends to give offence.
In troubles that cannot be avoided or trifling mishaps he will never cry
out or ask for help, since to do so would imply that he took them to
heart. He likes to own beautiful and useless things, rather than useful
things that bring in a return, since the former show his independence
more.

Other traits generally attributed to the great-souled man are a slow
gait, a deep voice, and a deliberate utterance; to speak in shrill tones
and walk fast denotes an excitable and nervous temperament, which
does not belong to one who cares for few things and thinks nothing [of
great importance].

Part Five

BETWEEN GREECE
AND ROME

Without realizing it Aristotle saw the end of the political importance of Athens and indeed of the city-states of Greece. His one-time pupil, Alexander of Macedon (356-323 B.C.), created a new kind of Greek world, a world of kingdoms and empires stretching from mainland Greece and Africa to India. It has been called in modern times the Hellenistic age. New intellectual centers—Alexandria in Egypt, Antioch in Syria, Pergamum in Asia Minor—vied with Athens. The intellectual atmosphere changed and developed. Philosophy and the sciences, still held in an uneasy union by Aristotle's metaphysics and scientific genius, took divergent paths soon after his death. Philosophers developed logic, ethics, and their own forms of physics; the natural sciences flourished independently. It was a golden age of specialization. Mathematics, mechanics, astronomy, geography, and medicine reached or approached levels which were not again equalled for almost 2000 years. Museums and libraries were organized; literary history had its beginnings; and poetry became increasingly the polished production of technically exacting works. Comparatively few examples have survived of Hellenistic Greek literature, and part of our knowledge of it comes from Roman imitations. In seeking to understand cultural developments at Rome it is important to realize that this was the Greek world with which Rome first came into contact.

As a new military power without much cultural background (in the Greek sense) Rome attracted little attention at first from the now largely eastern-oriented Greeks. But mastery of the western Mediterranean brought Rome into close contact with Greeks and face to face with the Hellenistic kingdoms. Here began Roman military and political conquest of the Greek world and the cultural Hellenization of Rome.

Greek slaves at Rome started to translate their own literature into Latin
and Romans began to imitate this civilization which was so much more
advanced than their own. After the defeat of Hannibal near Carthage
in 202 B.C. and of the kingdom of Macedonia 34 years later, a few cultured Greeks recognized the new importance of Rome and sought to influence her leading men or to explain to the Greek-speaking world her
rise to power. At Rome itself a number of prominent figures, symbolized
by the younger Scipio, took an increasing interest in Greek culture.

Polybius: The "Mixed Constitution" at Rome

Polybius lived at Rome for many years as a hostage after the Mace-
donian defeat in 168 B.C. and later was a companion of the younger
Scipio on his campaigns. He had excellent opportunity for observation and for collection of material, and he eventually used it to
write a history of Rome during the previous hundred years. The
avowed purpose of his work was to explain how this city was destined to conquer and rule over all other nations. The parts which
survive form one of the major remains of Hellenistic writing. His
historical method reflects the approach of a specialist, and there are
few better introductions to Roman civilization than those passages
in which he describes the Roman characteristics which he, as a
Greek, found most distinctive and effective. Although these are
concerned mainly with individual qualities of communal responsibility and patriotism, a group of famous chapters explains, in a
subtle application of Greek intellect to Roman realities, his theory
of the "mixed constitution" and the natural strength of the Roman
state.

The following excerpts from Polybius, *Histories* (6.3, 4, 9-11, 18
with omissions) are from the translation by W. R. Paton and are
reprinted by permission of the publishers from Loeb Classical Library, *Polybius*, Vol. III, Cambridge, Mass.: Harvard University
Press.

In the case of those Greek states which have often risen to
greatness and have often experienced a complete change of fortune, it is
an easy matter both to describe their past and to pronounce as to their
future. For there is no difficulty in reporting the known facts, and it is

not hard to foretell the future by inference from the past. But about the Roman state it is neither at all easy to explain the present situation owing to the complicated character of the constitution, nor to foretell the future owing to our ignorance of the peculiar features of public and private life at Rome in the past. Particular attention and study are therefore required if one wishes to attain a clear general view of the distinctive qualities of their constitution.

Most of those whose object it has been to instruct us methodically concerning such matters, distinguish three kinds of constitutions, which they call kingship, aristocracy, and democracy. Now we should, I think, be quite justified in asking them to enlighten us as to whether they represent these three to be the sole varieties or rather to be the best; for in either case my opinion is that they are wrong. For it is evident that we must regard as the best constitution a combination of all these three varieties, since we have had proof of this not only theoretically but by actual experience, Lycurgus having been the first to draw up a constitution—that of Sparta—on this principle. Nor on the other hand can we admit that these are the only three varieties; for we have witnessed monarchical and tyrannical governments, which while they differ very widely from kingship, yet bear a certain resemblance to it, this being the reason why monarchs in general falsely assume and use, as far as they can, the regal title. There have also been several oligarchical constitutions which seem to bear some likeness to aristocratic ones, though the divergence is, generally, as wide as possible. The same holds good about democracies. The truth of what I say is evident from the following considerations. It is by no means every monarchy which we can call straight off a kingship, but only that which is voluntarily accepted by the subjects and where they are governed rather by an appeal to their reason than by fear and force. Nor again can we style every oligarchy an aristocracy, but only that where the government is in the hands of a selected body of the justest and wisest men. Similarly that is no true democracy in which the whole crowd of citizens is free to do whatever they wish or purpose, but when, in a community where it is traditional and customary to reverence the gods, to honour our parents, to respect our elders, and to obey the laws, the will of the greater number prevails, this is to be called a democracy. We should therefore assert that there are six kinds of governments, the three above mentioned which are in everyone's mouth and the three which are naturally allied to them, I mean monarchy, oligarchy, and mob-rule. Now the first of these to come into being is monarchy, its growth being natural and unaided; and next arises kingship derived from monarchy by the aid of art and by the correction of defects. Monarchy first changes into its vicious allied form, tyranny; and next, the abolishment of both gives birth to aristocracy. Aristocracy by its very nature degenerates into oligarchy; and when the commons inflamed by anger take vengeance on this government for its unjust rule, democracy comes into being; and in due course the licence and lawlessness of this form of government produces mob-rule to complete the series. The truth of what I have just said will be quite clear to anyone who pays due attention to such beginnings, origins, and changes as are in each case natural. For he alone who has seen how each form naturally arises and develops, will be able to see when, how, and where the growth, perfection, change, and end of each are likely to occur again. And it is to the Roman constitution above all that this method, I think, may be successfully applied, since from the outset its formation and growth have been due to natural causes.

*   *   *

Such is the cycle of political revolution, the course appointed by nature in which constitutions change, disappear, and finally return to the point from which they started. Anyone who clearly perceives this may indeed in speaking of the future of any state be wrong in his estimate of the time the process will take, but if his judgement is not tainted by animosity or jealousy, he will very seldom be mistaken as to the stage of growth or decline it has reached, and as to the form into which it will change. And especially in the case of the Roman state will this method enable us to arrive at a knowledge of its formation, growth, and greatest perfection, and likewise of the change for the worse which is sure to follow some day. For, as I said, this state, more than any other, has been formed and has grown naturally, and will undergo a natural decline and change to its contrary. The reader will be able to judge of the truth of this from the subsequent parts of this work.

At present I will give a brief account of the legislation of Lycurgus, a matter not alien to my present purpose. Lycurgus had perfectly well understood that all the above changes take place necessarily and naturally, and had taken into consideration that every variety of constitution which is simple and formed on one principle is precarious, as it is soon perverted into the corrupt form which is proper to it and naturally follows on it. For just as rust in the case of iron and wood-worms and ship-worms in the case of timber are imbred pests, and these substances, even though they escape all external injury, fall a prey to the evils engendered in them, so each constitution has a vice engendered in it and inseparable from it. In kingship it is despotism, in aristocracy oligarchy, and in democracy the savage rule of violence; and it is impossible, as I said above, that each of these should not in course of time change into this vicious form. Lycurgus, then, foreseeing this, did not make his constitution simple and uniform, but united in it all the good and distinctive features of the best governments, so that none of the principles should grow unduly and be perverted into its allied evil, but that, the force of each being neutralized by that of the others, neither of them should prevail and outbalance another, but that the constitution should remain for long in a state of equilibrium like a well-trimmed boat, kingship being guarded from arrogance by the fear of the commons, who were given a sufficient share in the government, and the commons on the other hand not venturing to treat the kings with contempt from fear of the elders, who being selected from the best citizens would be sure all of them to be always on the side of justice; so that that part of the state which was weakest owing to its subservience to traditional custom, acquired power and weight by the support and influence of the elders. The consequence was that by drawing up his constitution thus he preserved liberty at Sparta for a longer period than is recorded elsewhere.

Lycurgus then, foreseeing, by a process of reasoning, whence and how events naturally happen, constructed his constitution untaught by adversity, but the Romans while they have arrived at the same final result as regards their form of government, have not reached it by any process of reasoning, but by the discipline of many struggles and troubles, and always choosing the best by the light of the experience gained in disaster have thus reached the same result as Lycurgus, that is to say, the best of all existing constitutions.

       *   *   *

The three kinds of government that I spoke of above all shared in the control of the Roman state. And such fairness and propriety in all respects was shown in the use of these three elements for drawing up the constitution and in its subsequent administration that it was impossible even for a native to pronounce with certainty whether the whole system was aristocratic, democratic, or monarchical. This was indeed only natural. For if one fixed one's eyes on the power of the consuls, the constitution seemed completely monarchical and royal; if on that of the senate it seemed again to be aristocratic; and when one looked at the power of the masses, it seemed clearly to be a democracy. The parts of the state falling under the control of each element were and with a few modifications still are as follows.

       *   *   *

Such being the power that each part has of hampering the others or co-operating with them, their union is adequate to all emergencies, so that it is impossible to find a better political system than this. For whenever the menace of some common danger from abroad compels them to act in concord and support each other, so great does the strength of the state become, that nothing which is requisite can be neglected, as all are zealously competing in devising means of meeting the need of the hour, nor can any decision arrived at fail to be executed promptly, as all are co-operating both in public and in private to the accomplishment of the task they have set themselves; and consequently this peculiar form of constitution possesses an irresistible power of attaining every object upon which it is resolved. When again they are freed from external menace, and reap the harvest of good fortune and affluence which is the result of their success, and in the enjoyment of this prosperity are corrupted by flattery and idleness and wax insolent and overbearing, as indeed happens often enough, it is then especially that we see the state providing itself a remedy for the evil from which it suffers. For when one part having grown out of proportion to the others aims at supremacy and tends to become too predominant, it is evident that, as for the reasons above given none of the three is absolute, but the purpose of the one can be counterworked and thwarted by the others, none of them will excessively outgrow the others or treat them with contempt. All in fact remains *in statu quo,* because any aggressive impulse is sure to be checked and from the outset each estate stands in dread of being interfered with by the others.

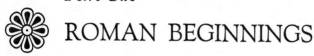

Part Six

ROMAN BEGINNINGS

The beginnings of Roman artistic and intellectual culture differed completely from those of Greece. There was, first of all, wholesale borrowing and imitation, at a comparatively late period, from another, highly developed civilization; secondly, there was no single figure at the very beginning whose pre-eminence continued, like Homer's, to influence all later literature and thought. The only vaguely comparable writer was Ennius, who came to Rome from south Italy and produced dramatic and other works in Greek style, but most importantly an epic of Roman history, the *Annals*, which adopted the meter of Greek epic. Strangely enough, the Roman ideal was usually caught most skilfully by non-Romans—few great Latin writers were born near Rome itself—and in Ennius' work the qualities of dogged perseverance, genial seriousness, pragmatic good sense, and unquestioning patriotism were pictured in a language appropriately forceful and lapidary. Such phrases as *moribus antiquis stat res Romana virisque* ("because of her traditions and her sons Rome stands secure") or (of Fabius against Hannibal) *cunctando restituit rem* ("by holding back he saved the state") remained vivid for later generations: wherever there was need for magniloquence, there were echoes of Ennius.

From the beginning Romans had mixed feelings about the Greeks and Greek culture. Admiration and imitation by some were balanced by distrust or contempt by others. Often the same person combined both attitudes. There was a conviction, shared by many foreign admirers, that there existed a simple Roman strength closely connected with the soil and with that devotion to one's gods and family and community which was known as *pietas*—this together with a pragmatic toughness which could be only adulterated by refinement or luxury. The adoption of Greek forms did not at all mean the eclipse of something distinctly Roman, but the eagerness and success of the adoption indicates that certain Greek elements had a special appeal to the Roman mind: adaptations of Greek drama were being produced and applauded by the dozen, though the comedies of Plautus and Terence were alone destined to survive. In this early period of experiment and conflict the old Roman ideal found an archetype in the elder Cato, while the comedies of his younger contemporary, Terence, gave a Latin form to some of those Greek ideals and manners which were later developed and most distinctly Romanized.

Plutarch: Portrait of Cato

It was a Greek, writing three centuries later, who collected the material which had gathered around the almost legendary figure of the elder Cato. His greatest fame had come from his repression of luxury and vice and his defense of traditional standards while holding the office of censor. Some accounts had made him intransigently anti-Greek, and unfriendly to the cultured circle of Scipio; others, probably more realistic, spoke of his Greek training and his admiration for Scipio. Plutarch includes all the conflicting versions, but throughout his portrait there runs a consistent thread of quick-witted toughness and patriotism which must have marked the man behind the legend.

The following excerpts from Plutarch, *Life of Cato* (1, 4, 19, 22, 23 in part) in the translation by Bernadotte Perrin, are reprinted by permission of the publishers from Loeb Classical Library, *Plutarch: Lives,* Vol. II, Cambridge, Mass.: Harvard University Press.

The family of Marcus Cato, it is said, was of Tusculan origin, though he lived, previous to his career as soldier and statesman, on an inherited estate in the country of the Sabines. His ancestors commonly passed for men of no note whatever, but Cato himself extols his father, Marcus, as a brave man and good soldier. He also says that his grandfather, Cato, often won prizes for soldierly valour, and received from the state treasury, because of his bravery, the price of five horses which had been killed under him in battle. The Romans used to call men who had no family distinction, but were coming into public notice through their own achievements, "new men," and such they called Cato. But he

himself used to say that as far as office and distinction went, he was indeed new, but having regard to ancestral deeds of valour, he was oldest
of the old.

*   *   *

The influence which Cato's oratory won for him waxed great, and
men called him a Roman Demosthenes; but his manner of life was even
more talked about and noised abroad. For his oratorical ability only set
before young men a goal which many already were striving eagerly to
attain; but a man who wrought with his own hands, as his fathers did,
and was contented with a cold breakfast, a frugal dinner, simple raiment,
and a humble dwelling—one who thought more of not wanting the super-
fluities of life than of possessing them—such a man was rare. The commonwealth had now grown too large to keep its primitive integrity; the
sway over many realms and peoples had brought a large admixture of
customs, and the adoption of examples set in modes of life of every sort.
It was natural, therefore, that men should admire Cato, when they saw
that, whereas other men were broken down by toils and enervated by
pleasures, he was victor over both, and this too, not only while he was
still young and ambitious, but even in his hoary age, after consulship
and triumph. Then, like some victorious athlete, he persisted in the regi-
men of his training, and kept his mind unaltered to the last.

*   *   *

It appears that the people approved of his censorship to an amazing
extent. At any rate, after erecting a statue to his honour in the temple of
Health, they commemorated in the inscription upon it, not the military
commands nor the triumph of Cato, but, as the inscription may be translated, the fact "that when the Roman state was tottering to its fall, he
was made censor, and by helpful guidance, wise restraints, and sound
teachings, restored it again." And yet, before this time he used to laugh
at those who delighted in such honours, saying that, although they knew
it not, their pride was based simply on the work of statuaries and paint-
ers, whereas his own images, of the most exquisite workmanship, were
borne about in the hearts of his fellow citizens. And to those who expressed their amazement that many men of no fame had statues, while
he had none, he used to say: "I would much rather have men ask why
I have no statue, than why I have one."

*   *   *

When he was now well on in years, there came as ambassadors from
Athens to Rome, Carneades the Academic, and Diogenes the Stoic philos-

opher, to beg the reversal of a certain decision against the Athenian people, which imposed upon them a fine of five hundred talents. The people of Oropus had brought the suit, the Athenians had let the case go by default, and the Sicyonians had pronounced judgment against them. Upon the arrival of these philosophers, the most studious of the city's youth hastened to wait upon them, and became their devoted and admiring listeners. The charm of Carneades especially, which had boundless power, and a fame not inferior to its power, won large and sympathetic audiences, and filled the city, like a rushing mighty wind, with the noise of his praises. Report spread far and wide that a Greek of amazing talent, who disarmed all opposition by the magic of his eloquence, had infused a tremendous passion into the youth of the city, in consequence of which they forsook their other pleasures and pursuits and were "possessed" about philosophy. The other Romans were pleased at this, and glad to see their young men lay hold of Greek culture and consort with such admirable men. But Cato, at the very outset, when this zeal for discussion came pouring into the city, was distressed, fearing lest the young men, by giving this direction to their ambition, should come to love a reputation based on mere words more than one achieved by martial deeds. And when the fame of the visiting philosophers rose yet higher in the city, and their first speeches before the Senate were interpreted, at his own instance and request, by so conspicuous a man as Gaius Acilius, Cato determined, on some decent pretext or other, to rid and purge the city of them all. So he rose in the Senate and censured the magistrates for keeping in such long suspense an embassy composed of men who could easily secure anything they wished, so persuasive were they. "We ought," he said, "to make up our minds one way or another, and vote on what the embassy proposes, in order that these men may return to their schools and lecture to the sons of Greece, while the youth of Rome give ear to their laws and magistrates, as heretofore."

This he did, not, as some think, out of personal hostility to Carneades, but because he was wholly averse to philosophy, and made mock of all Greek culture and training, out of patriotic zeal.

Terence: The *Self-Tormentor*

Later generations thought Terence's Latin as elegant as any ever written. Little is known of him. A foreigner, probably an African, he was for a few youthful years part of Scipio's circle, wrote six comedies adapted from Greek originals, then disappeared from view. His rather gentle comedies of manners, quite unlike the racy, often boisterous work of Plautus, show a remarkable sense of character and situation. The opening scene of his *Self-Tormentor* is a masterpiece of characterization and presentation of plot through dialogue. More importantly, it contains the earliest and the classic Latin statement of that sense of human interdependence and humane responsibility which was to become a leading theme of Roman civilization as its parochial values were transmuted into universal ones: *homo sum—humani nil a me alienum puto.*

The translation by John Sargeaunt of Terence, *Self-Tormentor* (*Heautontimoroumenos*) 53-167, is reprinted by permission of the publishers from Loeb Classical Library, *Terence*, Vol. I, Cambridge, Mass.: Harvard University Press.

[On a farm near Athens the aging MENEDEMUS is hard at work. His neighbour CHREMES speaks to him.]

CHREMES. Young as this acquaintance of ours is, starting in fact from your purchase of the farm next to mine, and I must admit there has been no more business between us, still there's something—it may be your goodness or may be your living next door, a thing which I reckon the half-way house to friendship—something which leads me to admonish you with the boldness of an intimate friend. It seems to me you are working too hard for your time of life, harder than your circumstances demand. Heaven and earth, man, what's your meaning? what's your object? You are sixty years old, if not more, at least I guess so. As for estate there is no one hereabouts has a better or one worth more. You have plenty of men to work it, yet, just as if you hadn't a single one, there you are, straining yourself to do *their* work. However early I go off in the morning, however late I come home in the evening, I always catch sight of you on your farm busy with a spade or a plough or carrying some burden. In a word you never ease off for a single moment, never spare yourself at all. That the work is no pleasure to you I am quite sure. You may say you are dissatisfied with the amount of work done on the place. If the energy which you use up in personal labour were spent in keeping your men to their work, you would make a better thing of it.

MENEDEMUS. Chremes, have you so much time to spare from your own affairs that you can attend to another man's with which you have no concern?

CHR. I am a man, I hold that what affects another man affects me. You may take it that I am offering advice or asking a question, which you like, so that if you are right I may do as you, if you are wrong I may scare you out of this.

MENE. I have got to do this; you may do what you find necessary for your own case.

CHR. Has any man got to torment himself?

MENE. I have.

CHR. If you have some cause of distress, I am sorry; but what is it? what's the trouble? Please tell me what grievous crime you have committed against yourself.

MENE. Oh! oh! [in tears]

CHR. Don't weep, tell me your trouble whatever it is: don't be reserved or afraid. Trust me, I say; you'll find I can help you either by consolation or by advice, possibly by direct assistance.

MENE. You would like to be told?

CHR. Yes, for the reason I have given you.

MENE. Then you shall.

CHR. Well but your mattocks, lay 'em down for the present; whatever your trouble, don't go on working.

MENE. No, no.

CHR. But what's your object?

MENE. Don't prevent me giving myself no moment's holiday from work.

CHR. No really, I will prevent you. [takes the mattocks]

MENE. Ah, that's wrong of you.

CHR. What? heavy as this? My good man!

MENE. I have deserved it.

CHR. Now say on. [lays them down]

MENE. I have an only son, a mere lad. Ah, what do I say? have a son? No, I had a son, Chremes; whether I have one now I can't tell.

CHR. How is that?

MENE. I will tell you. In Athens there is a foreigner from Corinth, an old woman of small means. My son fell desperately in love with her daughter, in fact was almost as good as married to her, all this without my knowledge. When I found it out, instead of handling the matter kindly, in the way I ought to have dealt with a stripling's lovesick heart, I took the violent line that is common with parents. Day after day I nagged at him. "So, Sir," I would say, "do you think you're to be allowed such liberties any longer in your father's life-time, and almost as good as marry a mistress? You're mistaken, if you think so, and you don't know your man, Clinia. I am ready that you should be called my son just so far as you do what befits you; if you act otherwise you will see me find the fitting way to deal with you. Ay, all this comes merely from such a want of employment. When *I* was young I didn't busy myself with love. No, Sir, I was off to Asia because of my lack of means, and there on service, active service, Sir, got both money and glory." At last matters came to this pass: the lad by having this perpetually and painfully dinned into him was overcome. He reflected that from years and experience I must know better than he did and could look out for him better than he could for himself. Off to Asia he went, Chremes, to take service with the king.

CHR. Do you mean it?

MENE. Yes, he started without a word to me and has been gone three months.

CHR. You are both to blame, not but what his enterprise shows respect, yes and spirit as well.

MENE. When I found it out from the friends in his confidence I returned home in dejection, completely upset and my mind tottering with distress. I sank into a chair: up run my servants and pull off my shoes. I see others bustling about, arranging the cushions and laying for dinner, every one zealously doing his best to ease my unhappiness. The sight set me thinking. "What? are all these men to be so solicitous on my account only, for my sole satisfaction? All these maids to look to my clothes? All this vast household expenditure to be for me only, while my only son, who should have shared the enjoyment equally, no, had more of it, since youth is the time for enjoyment—I have driven the poor boy out by my injustice, mine? I should account myself deserving indeed of any punishment, if I acted in that way. No, so long as he lives that pinched life over there, cut off from his country by my harsh acts, I shall punish myself all the time for his sake, toiling, pinching, accumulating, slaving, all for him." That's what I have been doing from that moment. I left no stick in the house, not a jar, not a curtain, I scraped everything together. The slaves, men and women, except those who could easily make up the cost of their keep by work on the farm, every one of them I put up to auction and sold. My house I advertised for immediate sale. So I got together about four thousand pounds and bought this bit of land. Here I keep myself at work. I have made up my mind Chremes, that I lessen my wrong to my son in proportion as I make myself miserable, and that I am not entitled to enjoy any pleasure here until he comes back safe and sound and can share it with me.

CHR. You, I think, have the spirit of an indulgent father and he would be a compliant son if he were handled with fairness and tact. As it was, you didn't really know him nor he you. Where this happens there people are not living openly. You never disclosed how much he was to you, and he never dared place in you the confidence which is a father's right. Had that been done, this would never have happened to you.

MENE. That is so, I own it, I have been grievously in fault.

CHR. Still, my friend, for the future I hope for the best and I am confident you will see him return safe and sound and that very soon.

MENE. Heaven grant I may!

CHR. Heaven will. Now if you don't mind—it's the village feast here to-day—I should like you to dine with me.

MENE. Impossible.

CHR. But why? Do pray spare yourself the least bit. Though he's away your son would like you to do so.

MENE. It's not fit that after driving him off to hard labour I should now shirk it myself.

CHR. You are determined?

MENE. Yes.

CHR. Good-bye then.

MENE. Good-bye.

Part Seven

ROME: THE
CONSEQUENCES OF POWER

By the mid-first century B.C. Roman arms and diplomacy had brought mastery of the Mediterranean and of most of the adjoining lands. North Africa and Spain were being conquered; Greece had been reduced a century before; Julius Caesar pushed as far as Germany and Britain; in the east Pompey was negotiating with Armenia, while Roman armies were engaging the Parthian empire on the upper Euphrates. Only Egypt remained so far untouched. Untold wealth—both in money and in works of art—had poured into Rome, often in the hands of corrupt officials. Great houses were built, huge tracts of land acquired. The city itself was swollen with a new population, the countrymen of Italy dispossessed by rich landowners and slave labor. To this new center of power came foreigners, now not only slaves, but Greek, Syrian, and Asiatic businessmen, politicians, and intellectuals. And it became common for educated Romans to travel to the older centers of culture. Hellenistic literature, rhetoric, philosophy, and science were being transplanted and naturalized. Varro collected materials for a universal encyclopedia; Lucretius preached the philosophy of Epicurus in epic verse; the "new poets" adopted Alexandrian canons of learning and polish; a whole series of orators and prose writers—including Julius Caesar—applied Greek rhetorical theory to Latin; Cicero's genius above all encompassed an enormous range of Greek culture and re-created it with a distinctly Roman stamp.

There was a dark side to the picture. This new world was being governed by the same machinery which had directed the simple affairs of the city alone, and it became increasingly clear that senate, consuls, comitia, and tribunes were not equal to the task. New wealth had brought a more violent division of classes, while larger armies and regional campaigns encouraged personal military loyalties. Vastly higher stakes had brought vastly greater means and corresponding rewards for bribery, daring, and seizure of power. For eight decades civil government at Rome and the life of Italy were marked by bloodshed and by the continual reality or threat of civil war. The genius of Julius Caesar secured the uneasy peace and order of one-man rule, only to be broken once again by his assassination at the hands of self-styled defenders of the "old order."

The Romans were peculiarly aware of responsibilities to family, gods, and personal connections. The awareness of these bonds was called *pietas;* their scrupulous observance, especially in regard to the gods, was called *religio.* The state itself was subject to the same kind of responsibilities. Perhaps it was the glaring breach of these bonds—the unscrupulous or bloody rivalry of brother against brother for wealth and power, the internecine struggles which tore the state—which made the first century B.C. so conscious of *pietas.* It is a theme in every kind of literature, and never was the adjective *impius* used so often as then, as thoughtful men expressed their anguish at the eclipse of their most fundamental values. Cicero's achievement seems all the more extraordinary in forging the cultural links of a new civilization in the very face of personal and political defeat.

Lucretius: The Nature of the Universe

The fundamentally apolitical philosophy of Epicurus seems the least likely of the Hellenistic philosophies to have attracted Romans. It may be a token of the disillusion with older standards that many prominent men in this period adopted a view which denied religion and the afterlife and made personal pleasure (intellectual and physical) the chief goal of living. One of the great monuments of Latin literature is the poem in which Lucretius—of whom little is known beyond what he himself tells—fervently explains the Epicurean view of nature and man. The passionate earnestness of its author gives life even to passages which describe Epicurus' atomic theory. Lucretius shows a new aspect of the Roman mind in his exalted devotion to the Greek founder of his faith and in his obsession with overcoming the fear of superstition and death. But as soon as he sets out to picture evil among men, as in the opening of

the third book, with typical Roman concern he sees it in terms of
broken faith and disregarded bonds.

Lucretius, *De Rerum Natura* 3.1-93, is reprinted from A. D.
Winspear, *The Roman Poet of Science* (New York: Russell and
Russell) by permission of the author.

Into thick darkness came of old bright light.
You do I follow, you, who brought the light
To show us what is good and bad in human life,
You do I follow, glory of the Grecian race,
And in your footsteps firmly plant my own.
Not that I want to rival you; affection makes me want to imitate.
How can a swallow vie with swans
Or kids with little tottering limbs
On race track vie with mighty practiced horse?
You are the father of my mind, discoverer of Nature.
From your books, O seer renowned,
You give a father's precepts in philosophy.
As bees in blooming meadows suck each flower,
So we your golden words repeatedly
We feed on them and find them golden,
Worthy of eternal life.
Soon as your thought, born of a godlike mind,
Began to thunder forth on Nature's laws,
Then all terrors from our spirit flee;
The ramparts of the world are torn apart.
I see the atoms' pageant streaming through the void.
The power of godhead is revealed,
The quiet untroubled haunts of deity,
Which are not shaken by the wanton winds,
Nor lashed from cloud with rain.
No snow falls white nor frost assails;
Cloudless the air that covers them, and heaven bounteously smiles,
While sky is bathed in light.
Nature supplies them all they need for tranquil life
And nothing ever mars 'their sacred everlasting calm.'
Guided by you we never catch a glimpse of Hell's recess.
Earth cannot block our vision. We can see
Whate'er goes on in space beneath our feet.
And so, thinking your thoughts
And with your guidance mastering science
A kind of godlike pleasure comes on me,
Pleasure and horror mixed,

Because your power of mind
Has left the works of Nature naked to my view.
   Now since I have discoursed on atoms and have shown
What kind they are, how different in shape,
And how, self-moved, they ever fly,
In motion everlasting e'er impelled,
And how from atoms every object can be made,
Now I must tear up by the roots and cast away
That fear of death,
That fear that sullies mortal life from end to end
And pours the murk of death on everything,
Leaves no man's pleasure pure and unalloyed.
For though men often say disease and infamy
More dreadful are than deepest depths of hell;
And though they hold that soul is blood or wind
(Whichever theory they are clinging to),
And so they claim they need not our philosophy,
Yourself can judge that this is done for pomp and arrogance
Rather than deep belief.
For these same men,
Exiled from country, banished from human sight,
Black with the blackest crimes, gnawed by a hundred cares,
Live all the same.
Wherever wretchedness and anguish places them,
They worship all the same,
Butcher their sleek black bulls and give their offerings
To guardian spirits of the dead.
Their troubles turn their mind to creed and cult.
And so it's good to watch men in adversity,
By mounting dangers pressed.
At times like these
Men pour their deepest thoughts from depth of breast.
The mask is torn away, the face remains.
Then too, the lust for power and place and wealth,
Motives which make men pass the bounds of law,
And join in crime and struggle night and day
With all their might to scale the heights of wealth,
These wounds of life are too much nurtured by the fear of death.
Men see that infamy and biting poverty
Are far removed from pleasant tranquil life,
A kind of lurking at the gate of death.
These things they want to flee, spurred by false fear.
And so in time of civil war they build their wealth.
Their lust for gold outruns all bounds.
In piling wealth they slaughter heap on slaughter.

With hardened heart they gloat when a brother dies.
A kinsman's banquet they both hate and shun.
Likewise from this same fear envy can wear them down.
This man, they see, has power,
While that one wins respect and walks in fair renown,
And I, they'll say, am doused in murk and mire.
Some die to win their statues and their fame.
And sometimes even through their fear of death
Hatred of light and life takes hold of men.
With heavy hearts they kill themselves,
Forgetting that the fear of death caused all their woes.
The fear of death makes one man sully honour,
Another crash through friendship's bonds,
Wanton, in short with every human tie.
Often have men, seeking to skirt the shoals of death
Played false to fatherland and parents, too.
Like tiny boys who tremble in the dark
And think that anything may come,
We also tremble in the light and shrink from things
That in themselves are no more terrible
Than what boys fear in dreams and fancy sure to be.
And so this darkened terror of the mind must be dispelled
Not by the rays of sun or gleaming shafts of day,
But Nature's laws, by looking in her face.

Catullus: The Sense of Love and Loss

Catullus, a native of Verona, in what was then still counted as part
of Gaul, is, like Lucretius, hardly known except through his own
work. Many of his poems, occasional verse or lyrics, give bits of
personal information. He appears to have arrived in Rome as a
very young man, to have joined a brilliant social set, and to have
adopted the poetic technique and the standards of polished elegance
then in vogue among followers of Hellenistic Alexandria. He became a master of the technique, but into his poems infused as well
a directness and vitality which have made his ill-fated affair with
"Lesbia" a classic of passion and despair. He seems to have lived
hardly more than thirty years, but in the slender volume which survived is great variety: ribald poems of friendship and abuse, political lampoon and literary critique, artful trifles and elegant hymns,

even a miniature epic. There would appear to be little of Roman institutionalism in so Hellenized and individualistic a poet. And yet it has been observed that in moments of deepest and most personal feeling—his self-pity and farewells to his passion, his gratitude to his friend Allius, his journey to his brother's grave—Catullus strangely reverts to the language and symbols of *pietas:* not mere love or faithlessness, but in Roman fashion the holy bonds or broken pledges of family and religion, even of the state.

The following selections from Catullus, *Carmina,* are translated by the editor.

109. You promise me, my life, that this our love will be happy and everlasting between us. Grant, great gods, that she have strength to keep this promise truly, and that she speak sincerely and from her heart, so that we may have power to keep through all our life this eternal compact of hallowed friendship.

72. You used to say, once, Lesbia, that you knew no one but Catullus, and not Jupiter would you embrace sooner than me. I loved you then, not just as the crowd loves a mistress, but as a father loves his sons and sons-in-law. Now *I* know *you:* and so, though I burn with a richer fire, you seem cheaper to me and less important. How can that be? you say. Because this sort of hurt makes a lover love the more, but cherish less.

76. If there's any joy to a man in recalling kindness he has done, when he considers that he has been true (*pius*), and has not broken sacred trust, nor in any human compact used the gods' majesty to deceive, there are many joys for you in a long life, Catullus, earned from this thankless love. For whatever kindness man can show to man by word or deed has been said and done by you—all entrusted to an unreturning heart, and lost.

Why still torment yourself? Why not make up your mind, draw back, stop being miserable (despite the gods)?

It is hard to lay aside in a moment a love that has lasted long.

It is hard; but somehow you must do it. This is the only salvation, this the thing to be conquered, this to be done, whether you have the power or not.

O gods, if you show mercy, if ever you brought help at the very last, look on me in my distress, and if I have been pure in life, take this plague and ruin from me. Alas! a sickness creeps through my inmost fibers, and has cast all joys from my heart. I ask no longer that she love me in return or—impossible wish—that she agree to be pure. I ask only to be well again and to lay aside this dreadful disease. Grant me this, you gods, as return for my goodness (*pietas*).

11 (lines 15-24). O my friends . . . take a little message, no kind one, to my mistress. Tell her to live long and flourish with her lovers, whom she holds, three hundred at a time, in her embrace, truly loving not a one, but tearing alike the guts of all.

And tell her not to look to my love as before—my love, which through her fault has drooped, like a flower at the meadow's edge, touched by the passing plow.

68b (lines 109-14). This gift of poetry—it was all I had—is given you, Allius, as return for many a kindness: lest this day and that, and another and another, touch your name with time's corroding rust. To this the gods will add those countless gifts which Themis long ago was wont to give to pious men of olden times. . . .

101. Voyaging through many lands and many seas I come, my brother, to this sad funeral rite, to present you with death's last honors, and to speak—in vain—to your silent ashes. For yourself has fate stolen from me, O my brother, so ruthlessly torn away! But yet accept these offerings the while, which by our fathers' custom have been handed down—sad tribute —as a last sacrament. Take them, wet with a brother's many tears, and for all eternity, my brother, hail and farewell.

Cicero: Idealism, Politics, and Eloquence

It is hard to do justice to Cicero in a brief space, not because of the depth of his achievement and his influence, but because of their breadth. Judgment of him, furthermore, will mark a difference between the political and the cultural historian. The former will condemn his failure to recognize political realities, the vanity which influenced his judgments, his hesitation and ineffectiveness at the most crucial moment. He not only failed to save the senate and the republic, but failed to ameliorate the circumstances of their demise. The cultural historian, on the other hand, will see a man who set out to make his native tongue expressive, and molded the cultivated language of western Europe; who sought to explain Greek philosophy and literary ideals to his countrymen, and became the major link between two worlds; who tried to formulate the principles and ideals of the Rome which he adored, and created a body of thought and example which clarified for his own and future centuries much of the best in Roman civilization.

Born in a small town near Rome, he occasionally spoke with wonder of his rise to position and influence as a lawyer and politician in the city. He was at first militantly anti-aristocratic, and as a "new man" he was always an outsider to the senatorial nobility with whom in politics he became eventually allied. The source of his strength and the place where he felt at ease was among the middle-class commercial stratum of *equites* ("knights"). He capitalized on this safe and conservative background not only in his theorizing about Roman politics but also in his popularization of Greek culture, which was still quite suspect. His training in Greek was excellent; his approach was not profound, but it was buoyantly enthusiastic and wide-ranging. His own philosophical position was not the Stoicism that one might have expected, but the scepticism and agnosticism which had been adopted by Plato's Academy.

Cicero's greatest contribution to Roman (and later) civilization was the cumulative definition and exposition throughout his works of his concept of *humanitas*. With a sure sense he saw that such a widening of the old Roman idea of fellowship and responsibility was true to his inherited standards and at the same time found theoretical support in his two major interests, Greek philosophy and Roman law. His work helped give "humanity" and "humanities" a sense which deepened subsequent Roman thought and, rediscovered at the Renaissance, enlightened the modern age.

I

In a speech defending the otherwise unknown Greek poet Archias, whose naturalized citizenship had been questioned, Cicero ends with a general defense of literature. It has long stood as a classic statement of humane values and particularly of the theory (inherited from Hellenistic Greece) of the two justifications of art—utility and pleasure. The phrase "broadening to the sympathies" in the short excerpts which follow translates the Latin adjective *humanus*.

Cicero, *Pro Archia Poeta* 12-14, 16, 23-24 (in part), translated by N. H. Watts, is reprinted by permission of the publishers from Loeb Classical Library, *Cicero: Pro Archia,* Cambridge, Mass.: Harvard University Press.

You will no doubt ask me, Gratius, to account for the deep interest I feel in my friend. It is because he provides refreshment for my spirit after the clamour of the courts, and repose for senses jaded by their vulgar wrangling. Do you think that I could find inspiration for my daily speeches on so manifold a variety of topics, did I not cultivate my mind with study, or that my mind could endure so great a strain, did not study too provide it with relaxation? I am a votary of literature, and make the confession unashamed; shame belongs rather to the bookish recluse, who knows not how to apply his reading to the good of his fellows, or to manifest its fruits to the eyes of all. But what shame should be mine, gentlemen, who have made it a rule of my life for all these years never to allow the sweets of a cloistered ease or the seductions of pleasure or the enticements of repose to prevent me from aiding any man in the hour of his need? How then can I justly be blamed or censured, if it shall be found that I have devoted to literature a portion of my leisure hours no longer than others without blame devote to the pursuit of material gain, to the celebration of festivals or games, to pleasure and the repose of mind and body, to protracted banqueting, or perhaps to the gaming-board or to ball-playing? I have the better right to indulgence herein, because my devotion to letters strengthens my oratorical powers, and these, such as they are, have never failed my friends in their hour of peril. Yet insignificant though these powers may seem to be, I fully realize from what source I draw all that is highest in them. Had I not persuaded myself from my youth up, thanks to the moral lessons derived from a wide reading, that nothing is to be greatly sought after in this life save glory and honour, and that in their quest all bodily pains and all dangers of death or exile should be lightly accounted, I should never have borne for the safety of you all the brunt of many a bitter encounter, or bared my breast to the daily onsets of abandoned persons. All literature, all philosophy, all history, abounds with incentives to noble action, incentives which would be buried in black darkness were the light of the written word not flashed upon them. How many pictures of high endeavour the great authors of Greece and Rome have drawn for our use, and bequeathed to us, not only for our contemplation, but for our emulation! These I have held ever before my vision throughout my public career, and have guided the workings of my brain and my soul by meditating upon patterns of excellence.

*　　　　*　　　　*

But let us for the moment waive these solid advantages; let us assume that entertainment is the sole end of reading; even so, I think you would hold that no mental employment is so broadening to the sympathies or so enlightening to the understanding. Other pursuits belong not to all times, all ages, all conditions; but this gives stimulus to our youth and diversion to our old age; this adds a charm to success, and offers a haven of consolation to failure. In the home it delights, in the world it hampers not. Through the night-watches, on all our journeying, and in our hours of country ease, it is our unfailing companion.

*   *   *

If anyone thinks that the glory won by the writing of Greek verse is naturally less than that accorded to the poet who writes in Latin, he is entirely in the wrong. Greek literature is read in nearly every nation under heaven, while the vogue of Latin is confined to its own boundaries, and they are, we must grant, narrow. Seeing, therefore, that the activities of our race know no barrier save the limits of the round earth, we ought to be ambitious that whithersoever our arms have penetrated there also our fame and glory should extend; for the reason that literature exalts the nation whose high deeds it sings, and at the same time there can be no doubt that those who stake their lives to fight in honour's cause find therein a lofty incentive to peril and endeavour. We read that Alexander the Great carried in his train numbers of epic poets and historians. And yet, standing before the tomb of Achilles at Sigeum, he exclaimed, "Fortunate youth, to have found in Homer an herald of thy valour!" Well might he so exclaim, for had the *Iliad* never existed, the same mound which covered Achilles' bones would also have overwhelmed his memory.

II

Hellenistic Greek philosophy had tended to extremes either of technicality or of belles-lettres and preaching. For two centuries the philosophies of Plato and Aristotle were half-forgotten even in their own schools. It was in contact with Rome that Greek thought regained its classic poise and Greece assumed the role of teacher and civilizer. And it was chiefly Panaetius, a half-heretical Stoic who abandoned the rigidity of his own school and made a conscious return to Plato, who assured Stoicism such influence at Rome. In his important discussions of the contemplative and the active life Cicero follows the congenial arguments of Panaetius.

Cicero, *De Officiis* 1.69-72, translated by Walter Miller, is re-

But there have been many and still are many who, while pursuing that calm of soul of which I speak, have withdrawn from civic duty and taken refuge in retirement. Among such have been found the most famous and by far the foremost philosophers and certain other earnest, thoughtful men who could not endure the conduct of either the people or their leaders; some of them, too, lived in the country and found their pleasure in the management of their private estates. Such men have had the same aims as kings—to suffer no want, to be subject to no authority, to enjoy their liberty, that is, in its essence, to live just as they please.

So, while this desire is common to men of political ambitions and men of retirement, of whom I have just spoken, the one class think they can attain their end if they secure large means; the other, if they are content with the little they have. And in this matter, neither way of thinking is altogether to be condemned; but the life of retirement is easier and safer and at the same time less burdensome or troublesome to others, while the career of those who apply themselves to statecraft and to conducting great enterprises is more profitable to mankind and contributes more to their own greatness and renown.

So perhaps those men of extraordinary genius who have devoted themselves to learning must be excused for not taking part in public affairs; likewise, those who from ill-health or for some still more valid reason have retired from the service of the state and left to others the opportunity and the glory of its administration. But if those who have no such excuse profess a scorn for civil and military offices, which most people admire, I think that this should be set down not to their credit but to their discredit; for in so far as they care little, as they say, for glory and count it as naught, it is difficult not to sympathize with their attitude; in reality, however, they seem to dread the toil and trouble and also, perhaps, the discredit and humiliation of political failure and defeat. For there are people who in opposite circumstances do not act consistently: they have the utmost contempt for pleasure, but in pain they are too sensitive; they are indifferent to glory, but they are crushed by disgrace; and even in their inconsistency they show no great consistency.

But those whom [n]ature has endowed with the capacity for administering public affairs should put aside all hesitation, enter the race for public office, and take a hand in directing the government; for in no other way can a government be administered or greatness of spirit be made manifest. Statesmen, too, no less than philosophers—perhaps even more so—should carry with them that greatness of spirit and indifference to outward circumstances to which I so often refer, together with calm of soul and freedom from care, if they are to be free from worries and lead a dignified and self-consistent life.

III

Cicero's most complete statement of his political sympathies comes in an aside during a courtroom speech defending Publius Sestius. The prosecution had referred slightingly to the "breed of aristocrats," the *optimates,* as they were called, who constituted one political faction at Rome. Cicero, who years before had had little sympathy with the nobility, attempts to generalize the name to include all good citizens, and speaks in passing of the sources of Roman civil unrest.

Cicero, *Pro Sestio* 96-102, translated by R. Gardner, is reprinted by permission of the publishers from Loeb Classical Library, *Cicero: Pro Sestio,* Cambridge, Mass.: Harvard University Press.

There have always been two classes of men in this State who have sought to engage in public affairs and to distinguish themselves in them. Of these two classes, one aimed at being, by repute and in reality, "Friends of the People," the other "Aristocrats." Those who wished everything they did and said to be agreeable to the masses were reckoned as "Friends of the People," but those who acted so as to win by their policy the approval of all the best citizens were reckoned as "Aristocrats." "Who then are these 'Best Citizens' of yours?" In number, if you ask me, they are infinite; for otherwise we could not exist. They include those who direct the policy of the State, with those who follow their lead. They include those very large classes to whom the Senate is open; they include Romans living in municipal towns and in country districts; they include men of business; freedmen also are among the "Aristocrats." In its numbers, I repeat, this class is spread far and wide and is variously composed. But, to prevent misunderstanding, the whole class can be summed-up and defined in a few words. All are "Aristocrats" who are neither criminal nor vicious in disposition, nor mad revolutionaries, nor embarrassed by home troubles. It follows, then, that those who are upright, sound in mind, and easy in circumstances are those whom you have called a "Breed." Those who serve the wishes, the interests and principles of these men in the government of the State are called the supporters of the "Aristocrats" and are themselves reckoned as the most influential of the "Aristocrats," the most eminent citizens, and the leaders of the State. What then is the mark set before those who guide the helm of state, upon which they ought to keep their eyes and towards which they ought to direct their course? It is that which is far the best and the most desirable for all who are sound and good and prosperous; it is "Peace with Honour." Those who desire this are all reckoned as "Aristocrats," those who achieve it as the foremost men and the saviours of the State. For just as it is unfitting for men to be so carried away by the honour of public office that they are indifferent to peace, so too it is unfitting for them to welcome a peace which is inconsistent with honour.

Now this "Peace with Honour" has the following foundations, the following elements, which our leaders ought to protect and defend even at the risk of life itself: religious observances, the auspices, the powers of the magistrates, the authority of the Senate, the laws, ancestral custom, criminal and civil jurisdiction, credit, our provinces, our allies, the prestige of our government, the army, the Treasury. To be a defender and an advocate of so many and so important interests requires an exalted spirit, great ability, and great resolution. For, in so large a body of citizens, there are great numbers of men who, either from fear of punishment, being conscious of their crimes, seek to cause revolution and changes of government; or who, owing to a sort of inborn revolutionary madness, batten on civil discord and sedition; or who, on account of embarrassment in their finances, prefer a general conflagration to their own ruin. When such men as these have found advisers and leaders for their vicious aims, storms are aroused in the commonwealth, so that those who have hitherto claimed possession of the helm of state must watch and strive with all their skill and devotion that they may be able, without any damage to those foundations and elements of which I have just spoken, to keep on their course and to reach that haven of "Peace with Honour." If I were to deny, gentlemen, that this course is stormy and difficult, perilous and treacherous, I should be telling a lie, the less excusable since not only have I always understood it to be so, but experience also has convinced me more than anyone else.

There are greater forces and means for attacking than for defending the State. The reason is, that reckless and abandoned men need only a

nod to set them moving, and their own natural disposition incites them
against the State; while honest folk somehow or other show less activity,
neglect the beginnings of movements, and are aroused to action at the
last moment only by simple necessity; so that sometimes, owing to their
hesitation and indolence, while they wish still to enjoy peace even with
the loss of honour, through their own fault they lose both. But among
those who have wished to be defenders of the State, the weaker desert,
the more timid are not to be found, those only remain firm and endure
everything for the sake of the State who are like your father, Marcus
Scaurus, who resisted all revolutionaries from Gaius Gracchus to Quintus
Varius, whom no violence, no threats, no unpopularity ever caused to
waver; or like Q. Metellus, your mother's uncle, who, in his censorship,
after he had placed his ban on L. Saturninus, a notable leader of the
popular persuasion, and after he had excluded from the list of citizens,
in spite of the violence of an excited mob, one who claimed to be a
Gracchus but was an impostor, and after he alone had refused to take an
oath to a law which he judged to have been illegally proposed, preferred
to renounce his country rather than his principles; or—not to recall so
many ancient examples, the number of which is worthy of the glory of
this Empire, and without mentioning by name any of the great men still
alive—such a man as Quintus Catulus lately was, whom neither danger's
stormy wind nor honour's gentle air could ever deflect from his course
either by hope or by fear.

Imitate these examples, I beg you in the name of the Immortal Gods,
you who aspire to honour, praise, and glory! These examples are glorious,
they are superhuman, they are immortal; they are proclaimed in common talk, are committed to the records of history, are handed down to
posterity. It is a difficult task; I do not deny it. There are great risks; I
confess it. Most truly has it been said,

> Many the snares that for the good are set,

but the poet adds:

> What many envy, many strive to win,
> For you to claim is foolishness, unless
> You summon all your toil and all your care
> To win it.

IV

After some years of enforced retirement Cicero was roused in his old age to political activity by the assassination of Caesar. He redeemed much previous indecision by his virulent resistance to Mark Antony and by his unflinching death. In a series of speeches known as Philippics (from their similarity to Demosthenes' speeches against Philip of Macedon) he recalls for the last time with moving eloquence the hopes and ideals of the republic.

Cicero, *Philippics* 2.112-119, translated by W. C. A. Ker, is reprinted by permission of the publishers from Loeb Classical Library, *Cicero: Philippics,* Cambridge, Mass.: Harvard University Press.

But let us disregard what is past and gone; the doings of this one day, this very present day, I repeat, this point of time in which I am speaking—defend them if you can. Why is the Senate hedged in by a cordon of armed men? Why are your henchmen listening to me sword in hand? Why do the doors of Concord not lie open? Why do you bring Ityraeans, of all tribes the most barbarous, down into the forum with their arrows? It is for his own protection he says he does this. Are not then a thousand deaths better than not to be able to live in one's own community without a guard of armed men? But that "protection," believe me, is none; it is by the affection and good will of your fellow-citizens you should be hedged, not by arms. The Roman people will wrest those arms from you, and wrench them out of your grip—may it be while we are still safe!—but in whatever way you deal with us, while you pursue your present policy you cannot, believe me, live long. For that consort of yours—of all wives the least illiberal, whom I portray without irreverence—has been too long a debtor to the Roman people for her third instalment. The Roman people still has men to whom to commit the helm of state: wherever they are, there is the State's every defence, or rather, the State itself, which so far has only avenged itself, and not restored its strength. It has, I say, assuredly young men of the highest birth ready to be its defenders: let them stay apart regardful of their ease as they choose, yet they will be recalled by the State. And the name of peace is sweet, and the thing itself wholesome, but between peace and servitude the difference is great. Peace is tranquil liberty, servitude the last of all evils, one to be repelled, not only by war but even by death. But if those our liberators have withdrawn themselves out of our sight, yet they have left the example of what they did. They did what no man had done. Brutus waged war against Tarquin who was a king when to be a king was lawful at Rome; Spurius Cassius, Spurius Maelius, Marcus Manlius, because of the suspicion that they aimed at kingly power, were put to death; the men of to-day were the first to attack with swords one not aiming at kingly power, but who was a king. That deed is not only in itself illustrious and godlike, but also set before us for our imitation, all the more because they achieved such a glory as seems scarce to be bounded by heaven itself. For although in the very consciousness of a splendid deed there was sufficient reward, yet by a mortal immortality should not, I think, be despised.

Recall therefore, Marcus Antonius, that day on which you abolished the dictatorship; set before your eyes the joy of the Senate and of the Roman people; compare it with this monstrous marketing conducted by you and your friends: then will you understand how great the difference between gain and glory. But assuredly, even as some, through a kind of disease and numbness of perception, do not perceive the flavour of food, so the lustful, the avaricious, the criminal, have no estimation of genuine glory. But if glory cannot allure you to right doing, cannot even fear call you away from the foulest deeds? The law-courts you do not fear. If because of your innocence, I praise you; but if because of your violence, do you not understand what he must be afraid of who in such fashion is not afraid of the law-courts? Yet if you have no fear of brave men and honest citizens because they are kept from your body by an armed guard, your own followers, believe me, will not endure you any longer. And what a life is it, day and night to dread your own followers? unless indeed you have men bound to you by greater favours than Caesar had in some of those by whom he was slain, or yourself are in any respect to be compared with him. In him there was genius, calculation, memory, letters, industry, thought, diligence; he had done in war things, however calamitous to the State, yet at least great; having for many years aimed at a throne, he had by great labour, great dangers, achieved his object; by shows, buildings, largesses, banquets he had conciliated the ignorant crowd; his own followers he had bound to him by rewards, his adversaries by a show of clemency: in brief, he had already brought to a free community—partly by fear, partly by endurance—a habit of servitude.

With him I can compare you in lust of domination, but in other things you are in no wise comparable. But out of very many evils which he has

flicted on the Commonwealth, there has emerged this much good: the
oman people has now learned how much to trust each man, on whom
• rely, of whom to beware. Think you not of these things? and do you
ot understand that it is enough for brave men to have learned how
eautiful in act, how grateful in benefit, how glorious in report, it is to
ay a tyrant? Or will men, when they did not endure him, endure you?
1 rivalry hereafter, believe me, they will hurry to do this work, and no
ow-coming opportunity will be waited for.

Recover your senses, at length, I beseech you; consider those from
hom you are sprung, not those with whom you live; treat me as you
ill; be reconciled to the State. But you must look to your own conduct;
or myself I will make my own profession. I defended the State in youth,
will not desert it in old age; I despised the swordsmen of Catiline, I will
ot dread yours. Aye, and even my body will I gladly offer if the liberty
f the State can be realised by my death, so that the anguish of the
oman people may some time bring to birth that with which it has so
ong travailed. For if nearly twenty years ago in this very temple I said
nat death could not come untimely to a consular, with how much
reater truth shall I say it in old age! By me indeed, Conscript Fathers,
eath is even to be wished for, now that the honours I have won and
ne deeds I have performed are past. These two things only I pray for;
ne, that in my death I may leave the Roman people free—than this no
reater gift can be given me by the immortal Gods—the other, that each
nan's fortune may be according to his deserts toward the State.

Sallust: The Strife of Factions

The work of Sallust is a useful corrective to Cicero's optimistic view
of the Roman nobility. A member of the popular party and a lieu-
tenant of Julius Caesar, Sallust amassed an enormous fortune by
corrupt means and was forced to retire from politics. He thereupon
set out to describe the strife-torn history of his era in a series of
monographs which consciously employed the mordant analyses and
sombre colors of Thucydides. In his works he showed the nobility
as chiefly responsible for the demoralization of political life at Rome.

Sallust, *Bellum Iugurthinum* 41-42, translated by J. C. Rolfe, is

reprinted by permission of the publishers from Loeb Classical Li
brary, *Sallust,* Cambridge, Mass.: Harvard University Press.

Now the institution of parties and factions, with all their at
tendant evils, originated at Rome a few years before this as the result of
peace and of an abundance of everything that mortals prize most highly
For before the destruction of Carthage the people and senate of Rom
together governed the republic peacefully and with moderation. Ther
was no strife among the citizens either for glory or for power; fear of
the enemy preserved the good morals of the state. But when the mind
of the people were relieved of that dread, wantonness and arroganc
naturally arose, vices which are fostered by prosperity. Thus the peac
for which they had longed in time of adversity, after they had gained i
proved to be more cruel and bitter than adversity itself. For the noble
began to abuse their position and the people their liberty, and ever
man for himself robbed, pillaged, and plundered. Thus the communit
was split into two parties, and between these the state was torn to piece

But the nobles had the more powerful organization, while the strengt
of the commons was less effective because it was incompact and divide
among many. Affairs at home and in the field were managed accordin
to the will of a few men, in whose hands were the treasury, the prov
inces, public offices, glory and triumphs. The people were burdened wit
military service and poverty. The generals divided the spoils of war wit
a few friends. Meanwhile the parents or little children of the soldier
if they had a powerful neighbour, were driven from their homes. Thu
by the side of power, greed arose, unlimited and unrestrained, violate
and devastated everything, respected nothing, and held nothing sacre
until it finally brought about its own downfall. For as soon as noble
were found who preferred true glory to unjust power, the state began t
be disturbed and civil dissension to arise like an upheaval of the earth.

For example, when Tiberius and Gaius Gracchus, whose forefather
had added greatly to the power of the republic in the Punic and othe
wars, began to assert the freedom of the commons and expose the crime
of the oligarchs, the nobility, who were guilty, were therefore pani
stricken. They accordingly opposed the acts of the Gracchi, now throug
the allies and the Latin cities and again through the knights, whom th
hope of an alliance with the senate had estranged from the common
And first Tiberius, then a few years later Gaius, who had followed i
his brother's footsteps, were slain with the sword, although one was
tribune and the other a commissioner for founding colonies; and wit

hem fell Marcus Fulvius Flaccus. It must be admitted that the Gracchi vere so eager for victory that they had not shown a sufficiently moderate pirit; but a good man would prefer to be defeated rather than to triumph over injustice by establishing a bad precedent.

The nobles then abused their victory to gratify their passions; they out many men out of the way by the sword or by banishment, and thus endered themselves for the future rather dreaded than powerful. It is his spirit which has commonly ruined great nations, when one party desires to triumph over another by any and every means and to avenge tself on the vanquished with excessive cruelty. But if I should attempt o speak of the strife of parties and of the general character of the state n detail or according to the importance of the theme, time would fail ne sooner than material.

Part Eight

ROME: DESPAIR AND A NEW HOPE

Peace and the beginnings of civil reform were ended by Caesar's death in 44 B.C. For Rome and the cities of Italy the struggle between Caesar's assassins and his political heirs, Mark Antony and the young Octavian, meant a renewed horror of internecine strife. At Rome Virgil in his youth could have seen Cicero's head and hands nailed to the rostrum from which he had so often spoken. A new flood of veterans was soon to drive from their lands citizens of the cities which had backed the wrong side. Everywhere there was disruption, fear, and bloodshed. Those many who had hoped for stability under Caesar took heart perhaps when his faction smashed the conspirators two years later at Philippi, but there began at once a rivalry between Octavian and Antony which seemed destined to renew the strife of the previous half-century. Passages in the poetry of Virgil and of Horace express the wavering hopes and terrors of this decade. For ten years an uneasy truce divided the Roman world— Antony having taken the richer prize of the East (where in Egypt he came under the influence of Cleopatra), Octavian being left with the problems of Italy, and Lepidus in Sicily—but in 31 B.C. Octavian, with a united Italy behind him, clashed victoriously with Antony and Cleopatra's fleet at Actium and in a few months was master of the world.

The forty-five years during which Octavian—known now as Caesar and Augustus—"reconstructed" the republic as a benevolently disguised one-man rule marks the climax of a golden age of Latin literature. Immense relief and gratitude for a moment of stability show themselves everywhere. The victory of Actium was pictured as a defeat of eastern irrationalism by the forces of order and law. Yet along with the praise and rejoicing comes a haunting pessimism—perhaps this generation had seen too much—and with it the haunting vision of a golden age. At times this longing for an era of rural tranquillity and simple faith was linked with the new order of Augustus (who encouraged such a belief), but more often it was a yearning for a peace and nobility lost in a distant past or recoverable only momentarily, perhaps in the countryside, at any rate far from centers of activity and power.

Virgil: The *Georgics* and the *Aeneid*

Virgil grew up in the countryside of northern Italy (which had been especially pro-Caesar), came to Rome, and eventually settled in the south near Naples. His connection with each part of Italy is in a way symbolic of his universality. No Latin writer was more imbued with Italian lore and history and more sensitive to the traditions and ideals of Rome, and yet none shows a more thorough knowledge of Greek literature and literary technique. A countryman who wrote of empire, a friend of Augustus who shunned the capital, a romantic in feeling and a formal technician, a literary genius who asked on his deathbed that his greatest work be burned—Virgil showed in his personality and methods the complexity which marks the insights and attitudes of his work. He has been called the panegyrist of Augustus, but his references to contemporary affairs were usually allusive and often ambiguous. He know the uses of power, but he never lost sight of its consequences. Virgil's unusual feeling for the world of nature and its intimate connection with men expresses a deeply ingrained Roman and Italian attitude which is found in a lesser degree in other writers. It is his high regard for all that is gentle and humble in life, his essential sympathy with the vanquished as well as with the victor, which makes him more the poet of humanity than the prophet of progress. In looking at the Roman world he recognized the glory of action, and its necessity, but he recognized them with tears.

I

The *Georgics* is ostensibly a long poem on farming. Like all Virgil's work, especially when he writes of nature, it has more than one level of reference. At the end of the first book a description of weather-signs blends imperceptibly into the prelude to quite another kind of storm, and a prayer for Octavian concludes with a terrifying picture of world disorder. The idea of some past guilt now being atoned, and of a savior who will end the atonement, are fateful themes which make their appearance in this period. The pessimistic tone of the ending is striking in a poem presumably published after Actium.

This passage, *Georgics* 1.461-514, is reprinted from *Virgil's Georgics* by S. P. Bovie, by permission of The University of Chicago Press.

In short, the sun will give you all the signs:
What promises the tardy dusk conveys,
From what direction wind drives tranquil clouds,
And what the dripping South Wind has in mind.
Does anyone dare say the sun is false?
He warns us when uprisings threaten blindly,
And furtive actions breed conspiracy.
He pitied Rome when Caesar was destroyed,
Concealed his radiant head in obscure gloom
And godless men feared everlasting night.
At that time, earth and sea, and baying hounds,
Uneasy birds, foreshadowed evil days.
How often we saw Aetna burst her bounds,
Hurling liquid rocks and fiery mass!
Germany heard weapons clash on high,
The Alps shook with a strange and fearful motion.
Uncanny voices sounded in the woods,
And ghastly phantom forms materialized.
The cattle uttered words (unspeakable!),
Streams stood still and chasms rent the earth;
Ivory statues wept, and bronze perspired.
The river Po swept through the woods with rage,
His maddened flood bore herds and barns away,
And omens darkened every sacrifice;
Blood flowed from wells, and through the lofty towns
Wolves' howling voices echoed all night long.
No other time has seen more flashes fall
From cloudless sky, more deadly comets blaze.
So once again the Roman battle lines
Clashed in civil war at Philippi;
The gods saw fit to fatten up once more
The plains of Macedonia with our blood.
And to those places there will come a day

When a farmer drives his curved plough through the earth
And strikes on Roman javelins worn with rust,
Or clinks an empty helmet with his spade,
And wonders at the massive bones laid bare.
O my country's gods, my homeland's heroes,
And Romulus, and Vesta, who protect
The Tuscan Tiber, Roman Palatine:
May our young Octavian Caesar right this world
That our disastrous age has overturned!
We have atoned in full for perjured Troy,
And long enough has heaven's court complained
That Caesar celebrates his triumphs here
On earth, where right and wrong have been reversed.
So many wars, so many shapes of crime!
The plough dishonored, fields left lying waste
Now that their men are drafted; curving scythes
Are pounded into shape for ruthless swords.
War in Germany, and in the East:
Neighboring towns dissolve their legal bonds,
And march across each other's boundaries.
Unholy Mars bends all to his mad will:
The world is like a chariot run wild
That rounds the course unchecked and, gaining speed,
Sweeps the helpless driver on to his doom.

II

Perhaps no other part of Virgil's work contains so many reflections
of his own and Roman attitudes as the eighth book of the *Aeneid*.
Aeneas, a refugee from fallen Troy, has come with his men after
years of wandering to the land which he is destined to inherit. Putting in near the mouth of the Tiber, he finds the countryside in
arms against him. He is told in a dream to seek help from King
Evander, who dwells upstream, and thus he visits the settlement
which will one day be the site of Rome. In this visit and its aftermath Virgil shows the full range of his abilities and sympathies: in
a bucolic mood he evokes his ideal of unpretentious heroism and of
Rome's original closeness to nature and the gods; he pictures briefly
the golden age; then he moves to a grander and more traditional
epic manner (though with a strong element of pathos—the youthful
Pallas is destined to die in battle) and at last, with echoes of Ennius,
to a triumphant close.

Virgil, *Aeneid* 8.306-731, is reprinted with the permission of Charles
Scribner's Sons from *The Aeneid of Virgil*, pp. 218-232, translated
by Rolfe Humphries (Copyright © 1951 Charles Scribner's Sons).

Then back to the city again; and old Evander
Kept his son Pallas near him and Aeneas,
Talking of various matters, so the journey
Was lightened, and the landscape charmed Aeneas,
Who wondered as he watched the scene, and questioned,
And learned its early legend. King Evander
Began the story: "Native Nymphs and Fauns
Dwelt in these woodlands once, and a race of men
Sprung from the trunks of trees, or rugged oak,
Men primitive and rude, with little culture:
They had no knowledge of ploughing, none of harvest;
The fruits of the wild trees, the spoils of hunting,
Gave them their nourishment. Then Saturn came here,
Fleeing Jove's arms, an exile from his kingdom.
He organized this race, unruly, scattered
Through the high mountains, gave them law and order.
He gave the place a name; Latium, he called it,
Since once he lay there safely, hiding in shelter.
Under his rule there came those golden ages
That people tell of, all the nations dwelling
In amity and peace. But little by little
A worse age came, lack-luster in its color,
And the madness of war, and the evil greed of having.
Then came the Ausonian bands, Sicanian peoples,
And the land of Saturn took on other names,
And the kings came, and the fierce giant Thybris
For whom we named our river; we forgot
Its older title, Albula. Here I came
An exile from my country, over the seas,
Driven by fate and fortune, which no man
Can cope with or escape. The nymph Carmentis,
My mother, led me here with solemn warnings
Under Apollo's guidance."
                                        So Evander
Finished the tale, resumed the walk. They came,
First, to an altar and a gate: Carmental
The Romans call it, in honor of that nymph
Who first foretold the greatness of the Romans,
The glory of Pallanteum. Past the portal
They came to a spreading grove, a sanctuary

Restored by Romulus, and under the cold cliff
The Lupercal, named, in Arcadian fashion,
For the great god Pan. And then Evander showed him
The wood of Argiletum, and told the legend
Of the death of Argus, once a guest. From there
They went to the Tarpeian house, and a place
Golden as we now know it, once a thicket,
Once brush and briar, and now our Capitol.
Even then men trembled, fearful of a presence
Haunting this wood, this rock. "A god lives here,"
Evander said, "What god, we are not certain,
But certainly a god. Sometimes my people
Think they have seen, it may be, Jove himself
Clashing the darkening shield, massing the storm-cloud.
Here you can see two towns; the walls are shattered,
But they remind us still of men of old,
Two forts, one built by Janus, one by Saturn,
Janiculum, Saturnia."

                         So they came,
Conversing with each other, to the dwelling
Where poor Evander lived, and saw the cattle
And heard them lowing, through the Roman forum,
The fashionable section of our city,
And as they came to the house itself, Evander
Remembered something, "Hercules," he said,
"Great victor that he was, bent head and shoulders
To enter here, and this house entertained him.
Dare, O my guest, to think of wealth as nothing,
Make yourself worthy of the god, and come here
Without contempt for poverty." He led him,
The great Aeneas, under the low rafters,
Found him a couch, nothing but leaves, and the bedspread
A Libyan bear-skin. And night came rushing down
Dark-wingèd over the earth.

                         And Venus' heart
Was anxious for her son, and with good reason,
Knowing the threats and tumult of the Latins.
She spoke to Vulcan, in that golden chamber
Where they were wife and husband, and her words
Were warm with love: "When the Greek kings were tearing
Troy's towers as they deserved, and the walls were fated
To fall to enemy fire, I sought no aid
For those poor people, I did not ask for weapons
Made by your art and power; no, dearest husband,

I would not put you to that useless labor,
Much as I owed to Priam's sons, however
I sorrowed for my suffering Aeneas.
But now, at Jove's command, he has made a landing
On the Rutulian coast; I come, a suppliant
To the great power I cherish, a mother asking
Arms for her son. If Thetis and Aurora
Could move you with their tears, behold what people
Unite against me, what cities sharpen weapons
Behind closed gates, intent on our destruction!"
So Venus pleaded, and as she saw him doubtful,
The goddess flung her snowy arms around him
In fondlement, in soft embrace, and fire
Ran through him; warmth, familiar to the marrow,
Softened his sternness, as at times in thunder
Light runs through cloud. She knew her charms, the goddess,
Rejoicing in them, conscious of her beauty,
Sure of the power of love, and heard his answer:
"No need for far-fetched pleading, dearest goddess;
Have you no faith in me? You might have asked it
In those old days; I would have armed the Trojans,
And Jupiter and the fates might well have given
Another ten years of life to Troy and Priam.
Now, if your purpose is for war, I promise
Whatever careful craft I have, whatever
Command I have of iron or electrum,
Whatever fire and air can do. Your pleading
Is foolish; trust your power!" And he came to her
With the embrace they longed for, and on her bosom
Sank, later, into slumber.
                              And rose early
When night was little more than half way over,
The way a housewife must, who tends the spindle,
Rising to stir and wake the drowsing embers,
Working by night as well as day, and keeping
The housemaids at the task, all day, till lamplight,
A faithful wife, through toil, and a good mother,
Even so, like her, with no more self-indulgence,
The Lord of Fire rose early, from soft pillows
To the labor of the forge.
                              An island rises
Near the Sicanian coast and Lipare,
Aeolian land, steep over smoking rocks.
Below them roars a cavern, hollow vaults
Scooped out for forges, where the Cyclops pound

On the resounding anvils; lumps of steel
Hiss in the water, and the blasts of fire
Pant in the furnaces; here Vulcan dwells,
The place is called Vulcania, and here
The Lord of Fire comes down. In the great cave
The smiths were working iron; a thunderbolt
Such as Jove hurls from heaven, was almost finished,
Shaped by the hands of Brontes, Steropes,
And naked-limbed Pyracmon. They had added
Three rods of twisted rain and three of cloud,
And three of orange fire and wingèd wind,
And now they were working in the flash, the sound,
The fear, the anger, the pursuing flame.
Elsewhere a chariot for Mars was building
To harry men and cities; and for Pallas
An awful shield, with serpent scales of gold,
Snakes interwoven, and the Gorgon's head,
Awaiting polish. The neck was severed, the eyes
Already seemed to roll, when Vulcan came
Crying, "Away with this! Another task
Demands your toil, your thought. Arms for a warrior!
Use all your strength, you need it now; exert
The flying hands, ply all your master skill,
Break off delay!" And all, obedient, bent
To the great task; the bronze, the golden ore
Run down like rivers, and the wounding steel
Melts in the furnace as they shape the shield,
Welding it, orb on orb, a sevenfold circle
Made one, for all the weapons of the Latins.
Some keep the bellows panting, others dip
The hissing bronze in water, and the anvil
Groans under the hammer-stroke. In turn they raise
Their arms in measured cadence, and the tongs
Take hold of the hot metal, twist and turn it.
So sped the work on Lemnos.

                                   And Evander
Was wakened by the kindly light of morning
And bird-song under the eaves, and the old man rose,
Donned simple tunic and sandals, and hung on
His simple sword, and over his shoulders twisted
The panther hide, out of the way of the hilt.
Two hounds were all his bodyguard; he came,
So, to Aeneas' cabin; he remembered
His words and promised service, found his guest
An early riser also; hand met hand,

And soon companions joined them, young prince Pallas,
Loyal Achates. They stroll a while, then settle
Themselves for conversation, and Evander
Is first to speak: "Great captain of the Trojans,
I cannot, while you live, consider Troy
A beaten town, I cannot see her people
As anything but victors. I am sorry
Our power to help is meager. On one side
A river hems us in, and on the other
Rutulian armies thunder at our walls.
Still, I can find you, or I think so, allies,
Great people, an encampment rich in kingdoms,
An unexpected aid. The fates have brought you
To the right place. Not far away, Agylla,
A city built of ancient stone, lies waiting,
A town the Lydians founded; you know the race,
Renowned in war. It was a prosperous city
For many years, until Mezentius ruled it,
A cruel, arrogant man, sadist and savage.
God pay him back in kind! I cannot tell you
All his foul deeds: this will suffice; he fastened
Live men to dead men, strapped their hands together,
Tied face to face, and killed them, slowly, slowly,
In the waste and stain and clasp of that long death.
They suffered long, his subjects, but at last
They rose in arms against him, his mad household,
Hurled fire to his roof-top, slaughtered his companions.
He fled that ruin to Rutulian fields,
Where Turnus' weapons shielded him. Now all
Etruria, risen in arms, demands,
With threat of war, the king for punishment,
And you shall be the leader of those thousands
Who throng the shore with ships, whose cry is *Forward!*
But an old prophet holds them back, those warriors,
The pride and glory of an ancient people,
Whom a just grievance and a righteous anger
Inflames against Mezentius. *It is not fated,*
He says, *for any native-born Italian*
To tame a race so proud. Choose foreign leaders!
And so the Etruscan battle-lines have settled
Unwarlike on the plain, through heaven's warning.
Tarchon himself has sent me envoys, bearing
The crown and sceptre, urging me to his camp,
Bidding me take the throne. But cold old age,
And years too thin for battle, these begrudge me

The high command. I would send my son, but Pallas
Comes from a Sabine mother; he is partly
A native-born Italian. You, Aeneas,
Possess the proper strength, the proper lineage,
The summons of the gods. Take up the burden!
My Pallas will go with you, my hope and comfort.
You are the one to teach him a soldier's duty,
How to endure; let him learn from you in action,
Behold your deeds, and, in his youth, admire them.
I will give two hundred horsemen, young Arcadians,
The flower of our manhood; and two hundred
Will go with you besides in the name of Pallas."

    Aeneas and Achates, listening, brooded
With downcast gaze, in troubled speculation
Prolonging bitter thoughts, but Venus gave them
A sign from the bright heaven: a flash of thunder
Came from the cloudless sky, a blare of trumpets,
And all things suddenly shaken. They looked up swiftly;
Again, again, they heard the roar and rumble,
They saw arms redden in the clear of heaven,
Listened to thunder in cloud. And some were frightened;
Not so the Trojan: he knew his mother's promise.
"Ask not, O friend, the meaning of the portent,"
He cried, "Olympus summons me; I know it.
This was the sign my goddess-mother promised
When war was near; she would bring me arms from Vulcan,
She said, to help us all. Alas! what slaughter
Waits for the Latins now! How costly, Turnus,
The price that must be paid me! Shields and helmets
And bodies of brave men, swept under Tiber.
Now let them call for battle, and break treaties!"

    He rose and at his quickening the altars
Blazed into sudden fire; he paid his honors
To Hercules, to all the gods of household,
And all made sacrifice, sheep duly chosen.
Aeneas sought, once more, his ships, his comrades,
Chose, to attend him, those most brave in battle,
Despatched the rest down stream again with tidings
To take Ascanius of his father's fortunes.
Horses are brought for all the Trojan leaders,
And for Aeneas the best, a charger, golden
With lion-skin caparison, claws gilded.

    And rumor flies about the little city
Spreading the news of horsemen on their mission
To Tarchon's shores, and mothers, in a panic,

Double their prayers, and fear comes nearer danger
With Mars' great image looming large. Evander
Holds Pallas by the hand, cannot release him,
Speaks through his tears: "If Jupiter would only
Bring me my lost years back, make me the man
I used to be, I was once, at Praeneste
Where I struck down the foremost ranks, and burned
The piled up shields! That day I was a hero,
A conqueror, and Erulus went down,
By this right hand, to hell. His mother gave him
Three lives, and threefold armor; I had to kill him
Three times, and did, and thrice I stripped his armor.
If I were what I used to be, my son,
They would never take you from me; and Mezentius
Would never have heaped those insults on his neighbor,
Never have made a widow of the city.
But you, great gods on high, and you, great king
Of the high gods, take pity on a father,
Hear the Arcadian king. I pray for life
As long as Pallas lives, I pray to see him
If you will spare him; if he comes back safely
I pray to meet him once again. No more
I ask; how hard my life may be, no matter.
But if there is in fortune any menace,
Something I cannot speak of, let me die
Before I know the worst, while I can hope
However I doubt, while still I have my Pallas,
My late and only pleasure, here beside me,
And never news for the worse!" And so they parted,
And servants helped the old man into the palace.
    They had gone from the gates, the horsemen, and Aeneas,
Achates and the Trojans, and in the centre
Pallas, a blaze of light, like Lucifer
Whom Venus loves beyond all fiery stars,
The glory risen from the ocean wave,
Dissolver of the shadows. On the walls
The mothers, trembling, watched them go, the squadrons
Bright in their bronze, and the cloud of dust behind them,
So, out of sight, where the road turns off to forest,
They go, the men in arms, and a shout arises,
And the column forms, and the echo of the gallop
Comes clopping back through the ground where the dust is rising.
    The cold stream, Caere, has a grove beside it,
Much reverenced of old, where the curve of the hills
And the dark firs make a shelter: the old people,

So rumor says, held grove and feast-day sacred
Here in Silvanus' honor, god of the fields,
God of the fold. Tarchon and his Etruscans
Were camped not far from here, and from the hill-top
Watchers could see their legions, tented safely
Through the wide plain. In Caere's grove Aeneas
Rested his horses and his weary warriors.

And the bright goddess through the clouds of heaven
Came bringing gifts, seeing her son alone
By the cold river in the quiet valley,
And spoke to him: "Behold, the gifts made ready
By Vulcan's promised skill. Fear not, my son,
To face the wars with Turnus and the Latins!"
After the word, the embrace. She placed the armor,
All shining in his sight, against an oak-tree;
Rejoicing in the gift, the honor, he turned
His eyes to these, over and over again,
Could not be satisfied, took in his hands
The helmet with the terrible plumes and flame,
The fatal sword, the breastplate, made of bronze,
Fire-colored, huge, shining the way a cloud,
Dark-blue, turns crimson under the slanting sun,
The greaves of gold refined and smooth electrum,
The spear, the final masterpiece, the shield.

Hereon the great prophetic Lord of Fire
Had carved the story out, the stock to come,
The wars, each one in order, all the tale
Of Italy and Roman triumph. Here
In Mars' green cave the she-wolf gives her udders
To the twin boys, turning half round to lick them,
And neither is afraid, and both are playing.
Another scene presents the Circus-games,
When Romans took their Sabine brides, and war
Broke out between old Tatius and the sons
Of Romulus, and was ended, monarchs pledging
Peace at the altars over sacrifice.
Mettus, the false, by the wild horses drawn
And quartered, sheds his life-blood over the brambles;
Porsena, the besieger, rings the city
For Tarquin's sake, exile and tyrant; Romans
Rush on the steel for freedom; Clelia breaks
Her bonds to swim the river; and Horatius
Breaks down the bridge. The guardian Manlius
Holds the high capitol and that crude palace
Fresh with the straw of Romulus; the goose

Flutters in silver through the colonnades
Shrieking alarm; the Gauls are near in darkness,
Golden their hair, their clothing, and their necks
Gleam white in collars of gold, and each one carries
Two Alpine javelins; they have long shields.
Near them, the Fire-god sets the priests with caps
Of wool, the miracle of the shields from heaven,
The Salii dancing, the Luperci naked,
And the chaste matrons riding through the city
In cushioned chariots. Far off, he adds
The seats of Hell, the lofty gates of Pluto,
Penance for sin: Catiline, with the Furies
Making him cower; farther off, the good,
With Cato giving laws. And all this scene
Bound with the likeness of the swelling ocean,
Blue water and whitecap, where the dolphins playing
Leap with a curve of silver. In the center
Actium, the ships of bronze, Leucate burning
Hot with the glow of war, and waves on fire
With molten gold. Augustus Caesar stands
High on the lofty stern; his temples flame
With double fire, and over his head there dawns
His father's star. Agrippa leads a column
With favoring wind and god, the naval garland
Wreathing his temples. Antony assembles
Egypt and all the East; Antony, victor
Over the lands of dawn and the Red Sea,
Marshals the foes of Rome, himself a Roman,
With—horror!—an Egyptian wife. The surge
Boils under keel, the oar-blades churn the waters,
The triple-pointed beaks drive through the billows,
You would think that mountains swam and battled mountains,
That islands were uprooted in their anger.
Fireballs and shafts of steel are slanting showers,
The fields of Neptune redden with the slaughter.
The queen drives on her warriors, unseeing
The double snakes of death; rattle and cymbals
Compete with bugle and trumpet. Monstrous gods,
Of every form and fashion, one, Anubis,
Shaped like a dog, wield their outrageous weapons
In wrath at Venus, Neptune, and Minerva.
Mars, all in steel, storms through the fray; the Furies
Swoop from the sky; Discord exults; Bellona,
With bloody scourge, comes lashing; and Apollo
From Actium bends his bow. Egypt and India,

Sabaeans and Arabians, flee in terror.
And the contagion takes the queen, who loosens
The sheets to slackness, courts the wind, in terror,
Pale at the menace of death. And the Nile comes
To meet her, a protecting god, his mantle
Spread wide, to bring a beaten woman home.
And Caesar enters Rome triumphant, bringing
Immortal offerings, three times a hundred
New altars through the city. Streets are loud
With gladness, games, rejoicing; all the temples
Are filled with matrons praying at the altars,
Are heaped with solemn sacrifice. And Caesar,
Seated before Apollo's shining threshold,
Reviews the gifts, and hangs them on the portals.
In long array the conquered file, their garments,
Their speech, as various as their arms, the Nomads,
The naked Africans, Leleges, Carians,
Gelonians with quivers, the Morini,
Of mortals most remote, Euphrates moving
With humbler waves, the two-mouthed Rhine, Araxes,
Chafing beneath his bridge.

                      All this Aeneas
Sees on his mother's gift, the shield of Vulcan,
And, without understanding, is proud and happy
As he lifts to his shoulder all that fortune,
The fame and glory of his children's children.

Horace: Shadow and Substance

Like Virgil, Horace was a countryman who never settled in the
capital and never surrendered to the bustling official life to which
he had ready access through his patron, Maecenas. He produced a
wide variety of poetry, but his four books of *Odes* have always most
fascinated men's minds. Like parts of Shakespeare, they sound occasionally like a tissue of quotations, so familiar is their phrasing, and
they give a deceptive impression of simplicity. Horace, again like
Virgil, has been called a propagandist poet and panegyrist of
Augustus, but that is a somewhat simple-minded view of one of the
most complex poets of European literature. Not only do laments
for the demoralization of Roman life follow close on poems prais-

ing Augustus and his minister, Maecenas, but even within the poems of praise there remains a certain reserve, and changes of attitude or direction will often qualify the compliment. Even simple odes of Horace show such shifts of mood that often one hardly knows whether the final effect is of sorrow or of joy. He too had yearnings for a golden age, and after the despair of civil war a new hope. But his too was an essential pessimism concerning power, lightened only by occasional visions of nobility expressed often in terms of the old Roman virtues. Behind the pessimism—itself half-veiled by a light-hearted manner—seems to lie a stubborn faith in the possibility of individual dignity and achievement. But this is far from the poetry of courtly praise.

A poetry whose effect comes from verbal subtlety and interplay of imagery and contrasting styles is hardly translatable. A single ode may best serve to indicate the typical complexity. In what begins as a standard "official" song of rejoicing at victory over the dreaded Egyptian queen—Antony is significantly omitted—the perspective suddenly changes half way through, and the ending dwells instead on the heroic nobility of her death.

Horace, *Carmina* 1.37, translated by C. E. Bennett, is reprinted by permission of the publishers from Loeb Classical Library, *Horace: Odes and Epodes,* Cambridge, Mass.: Harvard University Press.

Now is the time to drain the flowing bowl, now with unfettered foot to beat the ground with dancing, now with Salian feast to deck the couches of the gods, my comrades!

Before this day it had been wrong to bring our Caecuban forth from ancient bins, while yet a frenzied queen was plotting ruin 'gainst the Capitol and destruction to the empire,

with her polluted crew of creatures foul with lust—a woman mad enough to nurse the wildest hopes, and drunk with Fortune's favours. But the escape of scarce a single galley from the flames

sobered her fury, and Caesar changed the wild delusions bred by Mareotic wine to the stern reality of terror, chasing her with his galleys, as she sped away from Italy,

even as the hawk pursues the gentle dove, or the swift hunter follows the hare over the plains of snow-clad Thessaly, with purpose fixed to put in chains

the accursed monster. Yet she, seeking to die a nobler death, showed for the dagger's point no woman's fear, nor sought to win with her swift fleet some secret shore;

she even dared to gaze with face serene upon her fallen palace; courage-

ous, too, to handle poisonous asps, that she might draw black venom to
her heart,

   waxing bolder as she resolved to die; scorning, in sooth, the thought
of being borne, a queen no longer, on hostile galleys to grace a glorious
triumph—no craven woman she!

Livy: The History of Rome

Such was Livy's fame that in his old age, it is said, a Spaniard
from Cadiz travelled all the way to Rome merely to see him and,
having done so, returned home satisfied. Of the immense work in
which Livy traced in anecdotal detail the history of Rome from
its beginning till his own day, less than a quarter survives, and
much of it records the half-legendary accounts of Rome's earliest
age. It was just these accounts, however, and in particular the
story of Horatius Cocles, which Polybius had found so revealing of
the Roman character and source of power.

   Livy explains in his extraordinary preface—extraordinary for its
direct frankness and its pessimism—that of the various reasons for
writing history his was to trace the true character of Roman achievement. He had no interest in documentation and little concern for
historical accuracy, but the epic sweep and power of his work have
made it a source of unending interest and insight.

I

Livy, *Ab Urbe Condita* 1. Preface, translated by B. O. Foster, is
reprinted by permission of the publishers from Loeb Classical Library, *Livy*, Vol. I, Cambridge, Mass.: Harvard University Press.

Whether I am likely to accomplish anything worthy of the
labour, if I record the achievements of the Roman people from the
foundation of the city, I do not really know, nor if I knew would I dare
to avouch it; preceiving as I do that the theme is not only old but hack-
neyed, through the constant succession of new historians, who believe

either that in their facts they can produce more authentic information or that in their style they will prove better than the rude attempts of the ancients. Yet, however this shall be, it will be a satisfaction to have done myself as much as lies in me to commemorate the deeds of the foremost people of the world; and if in so vast a company of writers my own reputation should be obscure, my consolation would be the fame and greatness of those whose renown will throw mine into the shade. Moreover, my subject involves infinite labour, seeing that it must be traced back above seven hundred years, and that proceeding from slender beginnings it has so increased as now to be burdened by its own magnitude; and at the same time I doubt not that to most readers the earliest origins and the period immediately succeeding them will give little pleasure, for they will be in haste to reach these modern times, in which the might of a people which has long been very powerful is working its own undoing. I myself, on the contrary, shall seek in this an additional reward for my toil, that I may avert my gaze from the troubles which our age has been witnessing for so many years, so long at least as I am absorbed in the recollection of the brave days of old, free from every care which, even if it could not divert the historian's mind from the truth, might nevertheless cause it anxiety.

Such traditions as belong to the time before the city was founded, or rather was presently to be founded, and are rather adorned with poetic legends than based upon trustworthy historical proofs, I purpose neither to affirm nor to refute. It is the privilege of antiquity to mingle divine things with human, and so to add dignity to the beginnings of cities; and if any people ought to be allowed to consecrate their origins and refer them to a divine source, so great is the military glory of the Roman People that when they profess that their Father and the Father of their Founder was none other than Mars, the nations of the earth may well submit to this also with as good a grace as they submit to Rome's dominion. But to such legends as these, however they shall be regarded and judged, I shall, for my own part, attach no great importance. Here are the questions to which I would have every reader give his close attention—what life and morals were like; through what men and by what policies in peace and in war, empire was established and enlarged; then let him note how, with the gradual relaxation of discipline, morals first gave way, as it were, then sank lower and lower, and finally began the downward plunge which has brought us to the present time, when we can endure neither our vices nor their cure.

What chiefly makes the study of history wholesome and profitable is this, that you behold the lessons of every kind of experience set forth as on a conspicuous monument; from these you may choose for yourself and for your own state what to imitate, from these mark for avoidance what is shameful in the conception and shameful in the result. For the rest, either love of the task I have set myself deceives me, or no state was ever greater, none more righteous or richer in good examples, none ever was where avarice and luxury came into the social order so late, or where humble means and thrift were so highly esteemed and so long held in honour. For true it is that the less men's wealth was, the less was their greed. Of late, riches have brought in avarice, and excessive pleasures the longing to carry wantonness and licence to the point of ruin for one-self and of universal destruction.

But complaints are sure to be disagreeable, even when they shall per-haps be necessary; let the beginning, at all events, of so great an enter-prise have none. With good omens rather would we begin, and, if historians had the same custom which poets have, with prayers and en-treaties to the gods and goddesses, that they might grant us to bring to a successful issue the great task we have undertaken.

II

The expulsion (traditionally put at 510 B.C.) of the Tarquins, the Etruscan kings of Rome, brought into being the republic and made the word "king" utter anathema for 500 years. It was during their first attempt to return that one of the famous incidents of Roman legendary history occurred. In the version known to Poly-bius, Horatius did not survive his exploit.

Livy, *Ab Urbe Condita* 2.9-10 (in part), translated by B. O. Foster, is reprinted by permission of the publishers from Loeb Classical Li-brary, *Livy*, Vol. I, Cambridge, Mass.: Harvard University Press.

By this time the Tarquinii had sought refuge with Lars Por-sinna, king of Clusium. There they mingled advice and entreaty, now imploring him not to permit them, Etruscans by birth and of the same blood and the same name as himself, to suffer the privations of exile, and again even warning him not to allow the growing custom of ex-pelling kings to go unpunished. Liberty was sweet enough in itself. Un-less the energy with which nations sought to obtain it were matched by

the efforts which kings put forth to defend their power, the highest would
be reduced to the level of the lowest; there would be nothing lofty
nothing that stood out above the rest of the state; there was the end of
monarchy, the noblest institution known to gods or men. Porsinna, be
lieving that it was not only a safe thing for the Etruscans that there
should be a king at Rome, but an honour to have that king of Etruscan
stock, invaded Roman territory with a hostile army. Never before had
such fear seized the senate, so powerful was Clusium in those days, and
so great Porsinna's fame. And they feared not only the enemy but their
own citizens, lest the plebs should be terror-stricken and, admitting the
princes into the City, should even submit to enslavement, for the sake
of peace. Hence the senate at this time granted many favours to the
plebs. The question of subsistence received special attention, and some
were sent to the Volsci and others to Cumae to buy up corn. Again, the
monopoly of salt, the price of which was very high, was taken out of
the hands of individuals and wholly assumed by the government. Im
posts and taxes were removed from the plebs that they might be borne
by the well-to-do, who were equal to the burden: the poor paid dues
enough if they reared children. Thanks to this liberality on the part of
the Fathers, the distress which attended the subsequent blockade and
famine was powerless to destroy the harmony of the state, which was
such that the name of king was not more abhorrent to the highest than
to the lowest; nor was there ever a man in after years whose demagogic
arts made him so popular as its wise governing at that time made the
whole senate.

When the enemy appeared, the Romans all, with one accord, withdrew
from their fields into the City, which they surrounded with guards. Some
parts appeared to be rendered safe by their walls, others by the barrier
formed by the river Tiber. The bridge of piles almost afforded an en
trance to the enemy, had it not been for one man, Horatius Cocles; he
was the bulwark of defence on which that day depended the fortune of
the City of Rome. He chanced to be on guard at the bridge when Jani
culum was captured by a sudden attack of the enemy. He saw them as
they charged down on the run from Janiculum, while his own people
behaved like a frightened mob, throwing away their arms and quitting
their ranks. Catching hold first of one and then of another, blocking their
way and conjuring them to listen, he called on gods and men to witness
that if they forsook their post it was vain to flee; once they had left a
passage in their rear by the bridge, there would soon be more of the
enemy on the Palatine and the Capitol than on Janiculum. He therefore

warned and commanded them to break down the bridge with steel, with
fire, with any instrument at their disposal; and promised that he would
himself receive the onset of the enemy, so far as it could be withstood
by a single body. Then, striding to the head of the bridge, conspicuous
amongst the fugitives who were clearly seen to be shirking the fight, he
covered himself with his sword and buckler and made ready to do battle
at close quarters, confounding the Etruscans with amazement at his au-
dacity. Yet were there two who were prevented by shame from leaving
him. These were Spurius Larcius and Titus Herminius, both famous for
their birth and their deeds. With these he endured the peril of the first
rush and the stormiest moment of the battle. But after a while he forced
even these two to leave him and save themselves, for there was scarcely
anything left of the bridge, and those who were cutting it down called to
them to come back. Then, darting glances of defiance around at the
Etruscan nobles, he now challenged them in turn to fight, now railed
at them collectively as slaves of haughty kings, who, heedless of their
own liberty, were come to overthrow the liberty of others. They hesitated
for a moment, each looking to his neighbour to begin the fight. Then
shame made them attack, and with a shout they cast their javelins from
every side against their solitary foe. But he caught them all upon his
shield, and, resolute as ever, bestrode the bridge and held his ground;
and now they were trying to dislodge him by a charge, when the crash of
the falling bridge and the cheer which burst from the throats of the
Romans, exulting in the completion of their task, checked them in mid-
career with a sudden dismay. Then Cocles cried, "O Father Tiberinus,
I solemnly invoke thee; receive these arms and this soldier with propi-
tious stream!" So praying, all armed as he was, he leaped down into the
river, and under a shower of missiles swam across unhurt to his fellows,
having given a proof of valour which was destined to obtain more fame
than credence with posterity.

III

Throughout Rome's history an ability to find effective compromise and to maintain a sense of communal loyalty was her greatest
strength. An amusingly simple illustration of this is seen in the
account of an early clash between the senate and the people ending
in the foundation of a vitally important magistracy.

Livy, *Ab Urbe Condita* 2.32-33 (in part), translated by B. O. Foster, is reprinted by permission of the publishers from Loeb Classical Library, *Livy*, Vol. I, Cambridge, Mass.: Harvard University Press.

The senators became alarmed, fearing that if the army should be disbanded there would again be secret gatherings and conspiracies. And so, although the levy had been held by order of the dictator, yet because the men had been sworn in by the consuls they regarded the troops as bound by their oath, and, under the pretext that the Aequi had recommenced hostilities, gave orders to lead the legions out of the City. This brought the revolt to a head. At first, it is said, there was talk of killing the consuls, that men might thus be freed from their oath; but when it was explained to them that no sacred obligation could be dissolved by a crime, they took the advice of one Sicinius, and without orders from the consuls withdrew to the Sacred Mount, which is situated across the river Anio, three miles from the City.—This version of the story is more general than that given by Piso, namely that the Aventine was the place of their secession.—There, without any leader, they fortified their camp with stockade and trench, and continued quietly, taking nothing but what they required for their subsistence, for several days, neither receiving provocation nor giving any. There was a great panic in the City, and mutual apprehension caused the suspension of all activities. The plebeians, having been abandoned by their friends, feared violence at the hands of the senators; the senators feared the plebeians who were left behind in Rome, being uncertain whether they had rather they stayed or went. Besides, how long would the seceding multitude continue peaceable? What would happen next if some foreign war should break out in the interim? Assuredly no hope was left save in harmony amongst the citizens, and this they concluded they must restore to the state by fair means or foul. They therefore decided to send as an ambassador to the commons Menenius Agrippa, an eloquent man and dear to the plebeians as being one of themselves by birth. On being admitted to the camp he is said merely to have related the following apologue, in the quaint and uncouth style of that age: In the days when man's members did not all agree amongst themselves, as is now the case, but had each its own ideas and a voice of its own, the other parts thought it unfair that they should have the worry and the trouble and the labour of providing everything for the belly, while the belly remained quietly in their midst with nothing to do but to enjoy the good things which they bestowed upon it; they therefore conspired together that the hands should carry no food to the mouth, nor the mouth accept anything that was given it, nor the teeth grind up what they received. While they sought in this angry spirit to starve the belly into submission, the members themselves and the whole body were reduced to the utmost weakness. Hence it had become clear that even the belly had no idle task to perform, and was no more nourished than it nourished the rest, by giving out to all parts of the body that by which we live and thrive, when it has been divided equally amongst the veins and is enriched with digested food—that is, the blood. Drawing a parallel from this to show how like was the internal dissension of the bodily members to the anger of the plebs against the Fathers, he prevailed upon the minds of his hearers. Steps were then taken towards harmony, and a compromise was effected on these terms: the plebeians were to have magistrates of their own, who should be inviolable, and in them should lie the right to aid the people against the consuls, nor should any senator be permitted to take this magistracy. And so they chose two "tribunes of the people," Gaius Licinius and Lucius Albinus. These appointed three others to be their colleagues.

IV

The eventual defeat of Hannibal, one of the ablest generals of antiquity, after he had crossed the Alps and ravaged Italy for fifteen years, was comparable in the Roman historical imagination to the Greek defeat of Xerxes. For years Quintus Fabius Maximus had pursued the unpopular but effective strategy of harrying Hannibal's forces but not risking a pitched battle. And Hannibal had never dared a frontal attack on Rome, which had not been taken since a siege by Gauls in force 100 years before. In two successive years, however, consuls abandoned Fabius' policy, and the disasters of Lake Trasumennus and of Cannae were the result. Memory of the driving dust of Cannae lived on in Roman literature, and nowhere can one get a better sense of the tenacity and vitality of Rome than in her reaction to this defeat.

Livy, *Ab Urbe Condita* 22.43, 49-51, 54-55 (in part), translated by B. O. Foster, is reprinted by permission of the publishers from Loeb Classical Library, *Livy*, Vol. V, Cambridge, Mass.: Harvard University Press.

But when the same Lucanian, Statilius, had made a thorough reconnaissance beyond the camp and on the other side of the mountains, and had reported seeing the enemy on the march a long way off, then the question of pursuing him began to be debated. The consuls were each of the same mind as they had always been; but Varro had the support of almost everybody, Paulus of none except Servilius, the consul of the year before. The will of the majority prevailed, and they set forward, under the urge of destiny, to make Cannae famous for the calamity which there befell the Romans. This was the village near which Hannibal had pitched his camp, with his back to the Volturnus, a wind that brings clouds of dust over the drought-parched plains. Such a disposition was very convenient for the camp itself and bound to be particularly salutary when the troops formed up for battle, facing in the opposite direction, with the wind blowing only on their backs, and ready to fight with enemies half-blinded by the dust driven into their faces.

*   *   *

The rout was now everywhere complete. Seven thousand men escaped into the smaller camp, ten thousand into the larger, and about two thousand into the village of Cannae itself. These last were immediately cut off by Carthalo and his cavalry, for the village was not fortified. The other consul, whether by accident or by design, had not joined any throng of fugitives, but fled to Venusia with some fifty horsemen.

It is said that forty-five thousand five hundred foot and two thousand seven hundred horse were slain, in an almost equal proportion of citizens and allies. . . . The prisoners taken in this battle are said to have numbered three thousand foot-soldiers and fifteen hundred horsemen.

Such was the battle of Cannae, a calamity as memorable as that suffered at the Allia, and though less grave in its results—because the enemy failed to follow up his victory—yet for the slaughter of the army even more grievous and disgraceful. For the flight at the Allia, though it betrayed the City, saved the army: at Cannae the consul who fled was accompanied by a scant fifty men; the other, dying, had well-nigh the entire army with him.

*   *   *

Hannibal's officers crowded round him with congratulations on his victory. The others all advised him, now that he had brought so great a war to a conclusion, to repose himself and to allow his weary soldiers to repose for the remainder of that day and the following night. But Maharbal, the commander of the cavalry, held that no time should be lost. "Nay," he cried, "that you may realize what has been accomplished by this battle, in five days you shall banquet in the Capitol! Follow after; I will precede you with the cavalry, that the Romans may know that you are there before they know that you are coming!" To Hannibal the idea was too joyous and too vast for his mind at once to grasp it. And so, while praising Maharbal's goodwill, he declared that he must have time to deliberate regarding his advice. Then said Maharbal, "In very truth the gods bestow not on the same man all their gifts; you know how to gain a victory, Hannibal: you know not how to use one." That day's delay is generally believed to have saved the City and the empire.

*   *   *

But at Rome it was reported that not even these pitiful remnants of citizens and allies survived, but that the army with its two consuls was clean destroyed and all their forces blotted out. Never, save when the City had been captured, was there such terror and confusion within the walls of Rome. I shall therefore confess myself unequal to the task, nor attempt a narrative where the fullest description would fall short of the truth. The year before a consul and his army had been lost at Trasumennus, and now it was not merely one blow following another, but a calamity many times as great that was reported; two consuls and two consular armies had been lost, and there was no longer any Roman camp, or general, or soldier; Hannibal was master of Apulia, Samnium, and well-nigh the whole of Italy. Surely there was no other people that would not have been overwhelmed by a disaster of such vast proportions. Would you compare the disaster off the Aegatian islands, which the Carthaginians suffered in the sea-fight, by which their spirit was so broken that they relinquished Sicily and Sardinia and suffered themselves to become tax-payers and tributaries? or the defeat in Africa to which this very Hannibal afterwards succumbed? In no single aspect are they to be compared with this calamity, except that they were endured with less of fortitude.

Publius Furius Philus and Marcus Pomponius, the praetors, called the senate together in the Curia Hostilia, to consult about the defence of Rome; for they made no doubt that the enemy, after wiping out their armies, would be advancing to besiege the City, which was all that remained to do to end the war. But when, amid dangers at once so immense and so incalculable, they failed to think of even any tolerable plan of action, and were deafened with the cries and lamentations of the women, both the living and the dead—in the lack as yet of any announcement—being indiscriminately mourned in almost every house, then Quintus Fabius Maximus urged that light-armed horsemen be sent out along the Appian and Latin ways, and questioning those they met—for some there would surely be who had dispersed and made off in the rout—bring back word of the fortunes of the consuls and the armies, and if the immortal gods, taking pity on the empire, had spared any remnant of the Roman name, where those forces were; whither Hannibal had gone after the battle, what his plans were, what he was doing and was likely to do. To discover and ascertain these facts was a task, he said, for active youths; what the Fathers themselves must do, since there were not magistrates enough, was this: quell the panic and confusion in the City; keep the matrons off the streets and compel them each to abide in her own home; restrain families from lamentation; procure silence throughout the City; see that bearers of any news were brought before the praetors—every man must wait at home for tidings that concerned himself—and, besides this, post sentries at the gates, to keep anyone from leaving the City, and make the people rest all hope of safety on the safety of Rome and of its walls. When the tumult had died down, then the Fathers must be convened again and consider how to defend the City.

Part Nine

✿ ROME: THE DISILLUSIONS OF EMPIRE

Writing a century after the events, Tacitus told the story of Augustus' death and the failure to shake off one-man rule. From this point on Rome became in effect a monarchy, and the excesses of certain emperors—which is what the name "Caesar" came to mean—showed the resiliency of the new form. The worst were assassinated or deposed by stronger men, and the system continued. Excellent administrators and generals ensured a largely successful regime for almost 200 years. With the instinct for compromise and inclusion which had marked their early history the Romans extended their citizenship and recognized local dignities. Eventually men from all parts of the empire were sitting in the Senate, even becoming emperors, and men to whom the city was only a name were proud to call themselves Roman citizens. Within a century Rome was a teeming metropolis. Extremes of wealth and poverty, mixture of races and nationalities, the old Roman families largely wiped out and replaced by new Roman blood returning from the provinces or else pushed aside by the meteoric success of Greeks and Syrians—this was the life of the capital of the world.

Rome was not displaced as the cultural center of the empire: thinkers and artists, Latin and Greek alike, looked to her as their real or spiritual home. Amid all this mixture and change the Roman mind was remarkably tenacious of certain traditional themes. Greek philosophy, especially Stoicism, combined with native habits of thought to keep alive a love of liberty and to nourish a growing universalism. In many of the greatest writers the vision of a golden age persisted, but now receding far into an idealized countryside or primitivism, or into an idealized past which darkened in comparison all the colors of the present day. The simple optimism of a poet like Statius or the cheerful geniality of the

Plinys seem pale beside the masterful irony or denunciation of a Tacitus, Lucan, or Juvenal. For most of the world it was an era of peace, prosperity, and intellectual activity; but at Rome there was a sense of lost liberty, increasing courtly flattery, and talk, continual talk, of decadence.

Seneca: Human Liberty

As tutor to the young Nero and chief minister of state during the glorious early years of Nero's rule, Seneca had had experience enough of practical affairs. The noble manner in which he later took his life at Nero's order—recorded in detail by Tacitus—shows a character consistent with his Stoic profession and teachings. It was the interim which has led to much criticism: his tacit cooperation in Nero's first crimes and his accumulation of vast wealth while writing essays and tracts on such virtues as poverty and courage. His importance as a stylist and thinker was great in the ancient world, however, and enormous in the Renaissance and after. For us his clipped and artificially rhetorical style has little attraction, but his obsession with the meaning of liberty and his sense of universal humanity are important testimonies to developments in Roman thought. He, for example—alone among Romans prior to the Christians—condemns the gladiatorial shows. His comments on slavery, in a letter to his friend Lucilius, show what a distance some influential men at Rome had advanced toward a new era.

Seneca, *Epistulae Morales* 47, translated by R. M. Gummere, is reprinted by permission of the publishers from Loeb Classical Library, *Seneca: Epistulae Morales,* Vol. I, Cambridge, Mass.: Harvard University Press.

I am glad to learn, through those who come from you, that you live on friendly terms with your slaves. This befits a sensible and well-educated man like yourself. "They are slaves," people declare. Nay, rather they are men. "Slaves!" No, comrades. "Slaves!" No, they are unpretentious friends. "Slaves!" No, they are our fellow-slaves, if one reflects that Fortune has equal rights over slaves and free men alike.

That is why I smile at those who think it degrading for a man to dine with his slave. But why should they think it degrading? It is only because purse-proud etiquette surrounds a householder at his dinner with a mob of standing slaves. The master eats more than he can hold, and with monstrous greed loads his belly until it is stretched and at length ceases to do the work of a belly; so that he is at greater pains to discharge all the food than he was to stuff it down. All this time the poor slaves may not move their lips, even to speak. The slightest murmur is repressed by the rod; even a chance sound—a cough, a sneeze, or a hiccup —is visited with the lash. There is a grievous penalty for the slightest breach of silence. All night long they must stand about, hungry and dumb.

The result of it all is that these slaves, who may not talk in their master's presence, talk about their master. But the slaves of former days, who were permitted to converse not only in their master's presence, but actually with him, whose mouths were not stitched up tight, were ready to bare their necks for their master, to bring upon their own heads any danger that threatened him; they spoke at the feast, but kept silence during torture. Finally, the saying, in allusion to this same highhanded treatment, becomes current: "As many enemies as you have slaves." They are not enemies when we acquire them; we make them enemies.

I shall pass over other cruel and inhuman conduct towards them; for we maltreat them, not as if they were men, but as if they were beasts of burden. When we recline at a banquet, one slave mops up the disgorged food, another crouches beneath the table and gathers up the leftovers of the tipsy guests. Another carves the priceless game birds; with unerring strokes and skilled hand he cuts choice morsels along the breast or the rump. Hapless fellow, to live only for the purpose of cutting fat capons correctly—unless, indeed, the other man is still more unhappy than he, who teaches this art for pleasure's sake, rather than he who learns it because he must. Another, who serves the wine, must dress like a woman and wrestle with his advancing years; he cannot get away from his boyhood; he is dragged back to it; and though he has already acquired a soldier's figure, he is kept beardless by having his hair smoothed away or plucked out by the roots, and he must remain awake throughout the night, dividing his time between his master's drunkenness and his lust; in the chamber he must be a man, at the feast a boy. Another, whose duty it is to put a valuation on the guests, must stick to his task, poor fellow, and watch to see whose flattery and whose immodesty, whether of appetite or of language, is to get them an invitation for to-morrow. Think also of the poor purveyors of food, who note their masters' tastes with delicate skill, who know what special flavours will sharpen their appetite, what will please their eyes, what new combinations will rouse their cloyed stomachs, what food will excite their loathing through sheer satiety, and what will stir them to hunger on that particular day. With slaves like these the master cannot bear to dine; he would think it beneath his dignity to associate with his slave at the same table! Heaven forfend!

But how many masters is he creating in these very men! I have seen standing in the line, before the door of Callistus, the former master of Callistus; I have seen the master himself shut out while others were welcomed—the master who once fastened the "For Sale" ticket on Callistus and put him in the market along with the good-for-nothing slaves. But he has been paid off by that slave who was shuffled into the first lot of those on whom the crier practises his lungs; the slave, too, in his turn has cut *his* name from the list and in his turn adjudged him unfit to enter his house. The master sold Callistus, but how much has Callistus made his master pay for!

Kindly remember that he whom you call your slave sprang from the same stock, is smiled upon by the same skies, and on equal terms with yourself breathes, lives, and dies. It is just as possible for you to see in him a free-born man as for him to see in you a slave. As a result of the massacres in Marius's day, many a man of distinguished birth, who was taking the first steps towards senatorial rank by service in the army, was humbled by fortune, one becoming a shepherd, another a caretaker of a country cottage. Despise, then, if you dare, those to whose estate you may at any time descend, even when you are despising them.

I do not wish to involve myself in too large a question, and to discuss the treatment of slaves, towards whom we Romans are excessively haughty, cruel, and insulting. But this is the kernel of my advice: Treat your inferiors as you would be treated by your betters. And as often as you reflect how much power you have over a slave, remember that your master has just as much power over you. "But I have no master," you say. You are still young; perhaps you will have one. Do you not know at what age Hecuba entered captivity, or Croesus, or the mother of Darius, or Plato, or Diogenes?

Associate with your slave on kindly, even on affable, terms; let him talk with you, plan with you, live with you. I know that at this point all the exquisites will cry out against me in a body; they will say: "There is nothing more debasing, more disgraceful, than this." But these are the very persons whom I sometimes surprise kissing the hands of other men's slaves. Do you not see even this—how our ancestors removed from masters everything invidious, and from slaves everything insulting? They called the master "father of the household," and the slaves "members of the household," a custom which still holds in the mime. They established holiday on which masters and slaves should eat together—not as the only day for this custom, but as obligatory on that day in any case. They allowed the slaves to attain honours in the household and to pronounce judgment; they held that a household was a miniature commonwealth.

"Do you mean to say," comes the retort, "that I must seat all my slaves at my own table?" No, not any more than that you should invite all free men to it. You are mistaken if you think that I would bar from my table certain slaves whose duties are more humble, as, for example, yonder muleteer or yonder herdsman; I propose to value them according to their character, and not according to their duties. Each man acquires his character for himself, but accident assigns his duties. Invite some to your table because they deserve the honour, and others that they may come to deserve it. For if there is any slavish quality in them as the result of their low associations, it will be shaken off by intercourse with men of gentler breeding. You need not, my dear Lucilius, hunt for friends only in the forum or in the Senate-house; if you are careful and attentive, you will find them at home also. Good material often stands idle for want of an artist; make the experiment, and you will find it so. As he is a fool who, when purchasing a horse, does not consider the animal's points, but merely his saddle and bridle; so he is doubly a fool who values a man from his clothes or from his rank, which indeed is only a robe that clothes us.

"He is a slave." His soul, however, may be that of a freeman. "He is a slave." But shall that stand in his way? Show me a man who is not a slave; one is a slave to lust, another to greed, another to ambition, and all men are slaves to fear. I will name you an ex-consul who is slave to an old hag, a millionaire who is slave to a serving-maid; I will show you youths of the noblest birth in serfdom to pantomime players! No servitude is more disgraceful than that which is self-imposed.

You should therefore not be deterred by these finicky persons from showing yourself to your slaves as an affable person and not proudly superior to them; they ought to respect you rather than fear you. Some may maintain that I am now offering the liberty-cap to slaves in general and toppling down lords from their high estate, because I bid slaves respect their masters instead of fearing them. They say: "This is what he plainly means: slaves are to pay respect as if they were clients or early-morning callers!" Anyone who holds this opinion forgets that what is enough for a god cannot be too little for a master. Respect means love, and love and fear cannot be mingled. So I hold that you are entirely right in not wishing to be feared by your slaves, and in lashing them merely with the tongue; only dumb animals need the thong.

That which annoys us does not necessarily injure us; but we are driven into wild rage by our luxurious lives, so that whatever does not answer our whims arouses our anger. We don the temper of kings. For they, too, forgetful alike of their own strength and of other men's weakness, grow white-hot with rage, as if they had received an injury, when they are entirely protected from danger of such injury by their exalted station. They are not unaware that this is true, but by finding fault they seize upon opportunities to do harm; they insist that they have received injuries, in order that they may inflict them.

I do not wish to delay you longer; for you need no exhortation. This, among other things, is a mark of good character: it forms its own judgments and abides by them; but badness is fickle and frequently changing, not for the better, but for something different. Farewell.

Juvenal: Farewell to Rome

It may well be that the bitter humor and exaggerated violence of Juvenal's criticisms of Roman life are in part merely the tradition of satire. Probably similar passages in Seneca stem from a literary tradition as well. But the wonderful detail of Juvenal's pictures gives a vivid sense of what had happened externally to Rome, while the framework of his values shows the continuing life of the ideals and contrasts of an earlier age. It is hard, furthermore, to deny some presentiment of almost hopeless collapse in a community which could produce so powerful a critic. His work makes the attitudes of others more understandable.

In one of his most effective satires he has accompanied to a gate of the city a friend who has decided to leave Rome and live in the country near Cumae. The friend, as he says farewell, recounts at length the evils of the city which have forced him at last into self-imposed exile—the flattery, the foreigners, the gulf between rich and poor, even the daily (and nightly) dangers of the streets.

The following selections from Juvenal, *Satires* 3, are in the translation by John Dryden.

I haste to tell thee—nor shall shame oppose—
What confidants our wealthy Romans choose,
And whom I most abhor: To speak my mind—
I hate, in Rome, a Grecian town to find.

To see the scum of Greece transplanted here,
Received like gods, is what I cannot bear.
Nor Greeks alone, but Syrians here abound:
Obscene Orontes, diving under ground,
Conveys his wealth to Tiber's hungry shores,
And fattens Italy with foreign whores.
Hither their crooked harps and customs come;
All find receipt in hospitable Rome.
The barbarous harlots crowd the public place:
Go, fools, and purchase an unclean embrace,
The painted mitre court, and the more painted face.
Old Romulus, and father Mars, look down:
Your herdsman primitive, your homely clown,
Is turned a beau in a loose, tawdry gown.
His once unkempt and horrid locks behold
Stilling sweet oil, his neck enchained with gold,
Aping the foreigners in every dress,
Which, bought at greater cost, becomes him less.
Meantime *they* wisely leave their native land,
From Sicyon, Samos, and from Alaband,
And Amydon, to Rome they swarm in shoals—
So sweet and easy is the gain from fools.
Poor refugees at first, they purchase here,
And, soon as denizened, they domineer,
Grow to the great, a flattering, servile rout,
Work themselves inward, and their patrons out—
Quick-witted, brazen-faced, with fluent tongues,
Patient of labours, and dissembling wrongs.
Riddle me this, and guess him if you can:
Who bears a nation in a single man?
A cook, a conjuror, a rhetorician,
A painter, pedant, a geometrician,
A dancer on the ropes, and a physician—
All things the hungry Greek exactly knows,
And bid him go to heaven, to heaven he goes.
In short, no Scythian, Moor, or Thracian born,
But in that town which arms and arts adorn.
Shall he be placed above me at the board,
In purple clothed and lolling like a lord—
Shall he before me sign, whom the other day
A small-craft vessel hither did convey,
Where, stowed with prunes and rotten figs, he lay?
How little is the privilege become
Of being born a citizen of Rome!

*   *   *

Who fears in country towns a house's fall,
Or to be caught betwixt a riven wall?
But we inhabit a weak city here,
Which buttresses and props but scarcely bear;
And it's the village mason's daily calling
To keep the world's metropolis from falling,
To cleanse the gutters and the chinks to close,
And for one night secure his lord's repose.
At Cumae we can sleep quite round the year,
Nor falls, nor fires, nor nightly dangers fear,
While rolling flames from Roman turrets fly,
And the pale citizens for buckets cry.

       *   *   *

Return we to the dangers of the night:
And, first, behold our houses' dreadful height,
From whence come broken potsherds tumbling down,
And leaky ware from garret windows thrown—
Well may they break our heads, that mark the flinty stone.
It's want of sense to sup abroad too late,
Unless thou first hast settled thy estate.
As many fates attend, thy steps to meet,
As there are waking windows in the street.
Bless the good gods, and think thy chance is rare
To have a pisspot only for thy share.

       *   *   *

Farewell; and when, like me, overwhelmed with care,
You to your own Aquinum shall repair
To take a mouthful of sweet country air,
Be mindful of your friend, and send me word
What joys your fountains and cool shades afford.
Then, to assist your satires I will come,
And add new venom, when you write of Rome.

Tacitus: Empire and Servitude

For fifteen years Cornelius Tacitus, a senator and leading orator at Rome, endured in silence the tyranny of Domitian. After Domitian's death in A.D. 96 Tacitus recorded with devastating brilliance the history of the emperors and the empire from Augustus to his own day. The earlier work, the *Histories*, dealt with the more recent period, while his last years were devoted to the *Annals*, the period between Augustus and the death of Nero. Seeing the whole development at Rome as a tragedy of secretive tyranny and deepening servitude relieved rather by the histrionics than the reality of protest, he forged a new style, dramatic and abrupt, in which to portray the stupidity and vice, the weakness and false heroism, the hidden motive and occasional virtue of those times. With swift-moving narrative and incisive characterization he combined a sure feeling for historical fact, thus giving an authoritative picture of the main political and military events of all areas of the empire.

I

The opening chapters of the *Annals* give a lightning survey of Roman constitutional history, an explanation of Tacitus' purpose, and then the account of the last days of Augustus and the accession of Tiberius Nero (the emperor Tiberius). They are a masterful and suggestive interpretation of the imperial heritage in the light of traditional Roman standards of liberty and simplicity.

Tacitus, *Annals* 1.1-7, translated by John Jackson, is reprinted by permission of the publishers from Loeb Classical Library, *Tacitus*, Vol. II, Cambridge, Mass.: Harvard University Press.

Rome at the outset was a city state under the government of kings: liberty and the consulate were institutions of Lucius Brutus. Dictatorships were always a temporary expedient: the decemviral office was dead within two years, nor was the consular authority of the military tribunes long-lived. Neither Cinna nor Sulla created a lasting despotism: Pompey and Crassus quickly forfeited their power to Caesar, and Lepidus and Antony their swords to Augustus, who, under the style of "Prince," gathered beneath his empire a world outworn by civil broils. But, while the glories and disasters of the old Roman commonwealth have been chronicled by famous pens, and intellects of distinction were not lacking to tell the tale of the Augustan age, until the rising tide of sycophancy deterred them, the histories of Tiberius and Caligula, of Claudius and Nero, were falsified through cowardice while they flourished, and composed, when they fell, under the influence of still rankling hatreds. Hence my design, to treat a small part (the concluding one) of Augustus' reign, then the principate of Tiberius and its sequel, without anger and without partiality, from the motives of which I stand sufficiently removed.

When the killing of Brutus and Cassius had disarmed the Republic; when Pompey had been crushed in Sicily, and, with Lepidus thrown aside and Antony slain, even the Julian party was leaderless but for the Caesar; after laying down his triumviral title and proclaiming himself a simple consul content with tribunician authority to safeguard the commons, he first conciliated the army by gratuities, the populace by cheapened corn, the world by the amenities of peace, then step by step began to make his ascent and to unite in his own person the functions of the senate, the magistracy, and the legislature. Opposition there was none: the boldest spirits had succumbed on stricken fields or by proscription-lists; while the rest of the nobility found a cheerful acceptance of slavery the smoothest road to wealth and office, and, as they had thriven on revolution, stood now for the new order and safety in preference to the old order and adventure. Nor was the state of affairs unpopular in the provinces, where administration by the Senate and People had been discredited by the feuds of the magnates and the greed of the officials, against which there was but frail protection in a legal system for ever deranged by force, by favouritism, or (in the last resort) by gold.

Meanwhile, to consolidate his power, Augustus raised Claudius Marcellus, his sister's son and a mere stripling, to the pontificate and curule aedileship: Marcus Agrippa, no aristocrat, but a good soldier and his partner in victory, he honoured with two successive consulates, and a little later, on the death of Marcellus, selected him as a son-in-law. Each of his step-children, Tiberius Nero and Claudius Drusus, was given the title of Imperator, though his family proper was still intact: for he had admitted Agrippa's children, Gaius and Lucius, to the Caesarian hearth, and even during their minority had shown, under a veil of reluctance, a consuming desire to see them consuls designate with the title Princes of the Youth. When Agrippa gave up the ghost, untimely fate, or the treachery of their stepmother Livia, cut off both Lucius and Gaius Cae-

sar, Lucius on his road to the Spanish armies, Gaius—wounded and sick
—on his return from Armenia. Drusus had long been dead, and of the
stepsons Nero survived alone. On him all centred. Adopted as son, as
colleague in the empire, as consort of the tribunician power, he was pa-
raded through all the armies, not as before by the secret diplomacy of
his mother, but openly at her injunction. For so firmly had she riveted
her chains upon the aged Augustus that he banished to the isle of Planasia his one remaining grandson, Agrippa Postumus, who, though guiltless
of a virtue, and confident brute-like in his physical strength, had been
convicted of no open scandal. Yet, curiously enough, he placed Drusus'
son Germanicus at the head of eight legions on the Rhine, and ordered
Tiberius to adopt him: it was one safeguard the more, even though
Tiberius had already an adult son under his roof.

War at the time was none, except an outstanding campaign against
the Germans, waged more to redeem the prestige lost with Quintilius
Varus and his army than from any wish to extend the empire or with
any prospect of an adequate recompense. At home all was calm. The
officials carried the old names; the younger men had been born after
the victory of Actium; most even of the elder generation, during the civil
wars; few indeed were left who had seen the Republic.

It was thus an altered world, and of the old, unspoilt Roman character
not a trace lingered. Equality was an outworn creed, and all eyes looked
to the mandate of the sovereign—with no immediate misgivings, so long
as Augustus in the full vigour of his prime upheld himself, his house, and
peace. But when the wearing effects of bodily sickness added themselves
to advancing years, and the end was coming and new hopes dawning, a
few voices began idly to discuss the blessings of freedom; more were ap-
prehensive of war; others desired it; the great majority merely exchanged
gossip derogatory to their future masters: "Agrippa, fierce-tempered, and
hot from his humiliation, was unfitted by age and experience for so heavy
a burden. Tiberius Nero was mature in years and tried in war, but had
the old, inbred arrogance of the Claudian family, and hints of cruelty,
strive as he would to repress them, kept breaking out. He had been
reared from the cradle in a regnant house; consulates and triumphs had
been heaped on his youthful head: even during the years when he lived
at Rhodes in ostensible retirement and actual exile, he had studied nothing save anger, hypocrisy, and secret lasciviousness. Add to the tale his
mother with her feminine caprice: they must be slaves, it appeared, to
the distaff, and to a pair of striplings as well, who in the interval would
oppress the state and in the upshot rend it asunder!"

While these topics and the like were under discussion, the malady of

Augustus began to take a graver turn; and some suspected foul play on the part of his wife. For a rumour had gone the round that, a few months earlier, the emperor, confiding in a chosen few, and attended only by Fabius Maximus, had sailed for Planasia on a visit to Agrippa. "There tears and signs of affection on both sides had been plentiful enough to raise a hope that the youth might yet be restored to the house of his grandfather. Maximus had disclosed the incident to his wife Marcia; Marcia, to Livia. It had come to the Caesar's knowledge; and after the death of Maximus, which followed shortly, possibly by his own hand, Marcia had been heard at the funeral, sobbing and reproaching herself as the cause of her husband's destruction." Whatever the truth of the affair, Tiberius had hardly set foot in Illyricum, when he was recalled by an urgent letter from his mother; and it is not certainly known whether on reaching the town of Nola, he found Augustus still breathing or lifeless. For house and street were jealously guarded by Livia's ring of pickets, while sanguine notices were issued at intervals, until the measures dictated by the crisis had been taken: then one report announced simultaneously that Augustus had passed away and that Nero was master of the empire.

The opening crime of the new principate was the murder of Agrippa Postumus; who, though off his guard and without weapons, was with difficulty dispatched by a resolute centurion. In the senate Tiberius made no reference to the subject: his pretence was an order from his father, instructing the tribune in charge to lose no time in making away with his prisoner, once he himself should have looked his last on the world. It was beyond question that by his frequent and bitter strictures on the youth's character Augustus had procured the senatorial decree for his exile: on the other hand, at no time did he harden his heart to the killing of a relative, and it remained incredible that he should have sacrificed the life of a grandchild in order to diminish the anxieties of a stepson. More probably, Tiberius and Livia, actuated in the one case by fear, and in the other by stepmotherly dislike, hurriedly procured the murder of a youth whom they suspected and detested. To the centurion who brought the usual military report, that his instructions had been carried out, the emperor rejoined that he had given no instructions and the deed would have to be accounted for in the senate. The remark came to the ears of Sallustius Crispus. A partner in the imperial secrets—it was he who had forwarded the note to the tribune—he feared the charge might be fastened on himself, with the risks equally great whether he spoke the truth or lied. He therefore advised Livia not to publish the mysteries of the palace, the counsels of her friends, the services of the soldiery; and also to watch that Tiberius did not weaken the powers of the throne by referring everything and all things to the senate: "It was a condition of sovereignty that the account balanced only if rendered to a single auditor."

At Rome, however, consuls, senators, and knights were rushing into slavery. The more exalted the personage, the grosser his hypocrisy and his haste—his lineaments adjusted so as to betray neither cheerfulness at the exit nor undue depression at the entry of a prince; his tears blent with joy, his regrets with adulation. The consuls, Sextus Pompeius and Sextus Appuleius, first took the oath of allegiance to Tiberius Caesar. It was taken in their presence by Seius Strabo and Gaius Turranius, chiefs respectively of the praetorian cohorts and the corn department. The senators, the soldiers, and the populace followed. For in every action of Tiberius the first step had to be taken by the consuls, as though the old republic were in being, and himself undecided whether to reign or no. Even his edict convening the Fathers to the senate-house was issued simply beneath the tribunician title which he had received under Augustus. It was a laconic document of very modest purport: "He intended to provide for the last honours to his father, whose body he could not leave—it was the one function of the state which he made bold to exercise." Yet, on the passing of Augustus he had given the watchword to the praetorian cohorts as Imperator; he had the sentries, the men-at-arms, and the other appurtenances of a court; soldiers conducted him to the forum, soldiers to the curia; he dispatched letters to the armies as if the principate was already in his grasp; and nowhere manifested the least hesitation, except when speaking in the senate. The chief reason was his fear that Germanicus—backed by so many legions, the vast reserves of the provinces, and a wonderful popularity with the nation—might prefer the ownership to the reversion of a throne. He paid public opinion, too, the compliment of wishing to be regarded as the called and chosen of the state, rather than as the interloper who had wormed his way to power with the help of connubial intrigues and a senile act of adoption. It was realized later that his coyness had been assumed with the further object of gaining an insight into the feelings of the aristocracy: for all the while he was distorting words and looks into crimes and storing them in his memory.

II

In Tacitus' short biography of his father-in-law, Agricola, the conqueror of northern Britain, there occurs a remarkably effective denunciation of Roman rule put into the mouth of a British chieftain just before Agricola's final victory. The speech is a rhetorical fiction, but written with such power that it leaves an unforgettably critical impression of the work of empire.

Tacitus, *Agricola* 29-32, is in the translation by A. J. Church and W. J. Brodribb.

Meanwhile, among the many leaders, one superior to the rest in valour and in birth, Galgacus by name, is said to have thus harangued the multitude gathered around him and clamouring for battle:

"Whenever I consider the origin of this war and the necessities of our position, I have a sure confidence that this day, and this union of yours, will be the beginning of freedom to the whole of Britain. To all of us slavery is a thing unknown; there are no lands beyond us, and even the sea is not safe, menaced as we are by a Roman fleet. And thus in war and battle, in which the brave find glory, even the coward will find safety. Former contests, in which, with varying fortune, the Romans were resisted, still left in us a last hope of succour, inasmuch as being the most renowned nation of Britain, dwelling in the very heart of the country, and out of sight of the shores of the conquered, we could keep even our eyes unpolluted by the contagion of slavery. To us who dwell on the uttermost confines of the earth and of freedom, this remote sanctuary of Britain's glory has up to this time been a defence. Now, however, the furthest limits of Britain are thrown open, and the unknown always passes for the marvellous. But there are no tribes beyond us, nothing indeed but waves and rocks, and the yet more terrible Romans, from whose oppression escape is vainly sought by obedience and submission. Robbers of the world, having by their universal plunder exhausted the land, they rifle the deep. If the enemy be rich, they are rapacious; if he be poor, they lust for dominion; neither the east nor the west has been able to satisfy them. Alone among men they covet with equal eagerness poverty and riches. To robbery, slaughter, plunder, they give the lying name of empire; they make a solitude and call it peace.

"Nature has willed that every man's children and kindred should be his dearest objects. Yet these are torn from us by conscriptions to be slaves elsewhere. Our wives and our sisters, even though they may escape violation from the enemy, are dishonoured under the names of friendship and hospitality. Our goods and fortunes they collect for their tribute, our harvests for their granaries. Our very hands and bodies, under the lash and in the midst of insult, are worn down by the toil of clearing forests and morasses. Creatures born to slavery are sold once for all, and are, moreover, fed by their masters; but Britain is daily purchasing, is daily feeding, her own enslaved people. And as in a household the last comer among the slaves is always the butt of his companions, so we in a world long used to slavery, as the newest and the most contemptible, are marked out for destruction. We have neither fruitful plains, nor mines, nor harbours, for the working of which we may be spared. Valour, too, and high spirit in subjects, are offensive to rulers; besides, remoteness and seclusion, while they give safety, provoke suspicion. Since then you cannot hope for quarter, take courage, I beseech you, whether it be safety or renown that you hold most precious. Under a woman's leadership the Brigantes were able to burn a colony, to storm a camp, and had not success ended in supineness, might have thrown off the yoke. Let us, then, a fresh and unconquered people, never likely to abuse our freedom, show forthwith at the very first onset what heroes Caledonia has in reserve.

"Do you suppose that the Romans will be as brave in war as they are licentious in peace? To our strifes and discords they owe their fame, and they turn the errors of an enemy to the renown of their own army, an army which, composed as it is of every variety of nations, is held together by success and will be broken up by disaster. These Gauls and Germans, and, I blush to say, these numerous Britons, who, though they lend their lives to support a stranger's rule, have been its enemies longer than its subjects, you cannot imagine to be bound by fidelity and affection. Fear and terror there certainly are, feeble bonds of attachment; remove them, and those who have ceased to fear will begin to hate. All the incentives to victory are on our side. The Romans have no wives to kindle their courage; no parents to taunt them with flight; many have either no country or one far away. Few in number, dismayed by their ignorance, looking around upon a sky, a sea, and forests which are all unfamiliar to them; hemmed in, as it were, and enmeshed, the Gods have delivered them into our hands. Be not frightened by idle display, by the glitter of gold and of silver, which can neither protect nor wound. In the very ranks of the enemy we shall find our own forces. Britons will acknowledge their own cause; Gauls will remember past freedom; the other Germans will abandon them, as but lately did the Usipii. Behind them there is nothing to dread. The forts are ungarrisoned; the colonies in the hands of aged men; what with disloyal subjects and oppressive rulers, the towns are ill-affected and rife with discord. On the one side you have a general and an army; on the other, tribute, the mines, and all the other penalties of an enslaved people. Whether you endure these for ever, or instantly avenge them, this field is to decide. Think, therefore, as you advance to battle, at once of your ancestors and of your posterity."

Part Ten

EPILOGUE: THE RULE OF ROMAN LAW

It would be unrealistic to end with a wholly critical account of Roman imperial rule. Of its many lasting benefits none is more important than the creation of a highly developed system of justice and law. In Cicero's time it had already had a long history, and he was in a position to clarify its principles. Six centuries later the emperor Justinian ordered a complete compilation and summary of the body and principles of law in a group of works which were henceforth a foundation stone of European ideas of justice and humanity.

I

The first selection, Cicero, *De Officiis* 1.20-23, 50-51 (in part), translated by Walter Miller, is reprinted by permission of the publishers from Loeb Classical Library, *Cicero: De Officiis,* Cambridge, Mass.: Harvard University Press.

Of the three remaining divisions, the most extensive in its application is the principle by which society and what we may call its "common bonds" are maintained. Of this again there are two divisions—justice, in which is the crowning glory of the virtues and on the basis of which men are called "good men"; and, close akin to justice, charity, which may also be called kindness or generosity.

The first office of justice is to keep one man from doing harm to another, unless provoked by wrong; and the next is to lead men to use common possessions for the common interests, private property for their own.

There is, however, no such thing as private ownership established by nature, but property becomes private either through long occupancy (as in the case of those who long ago settled in unoccupied territory) or through conquest (as in the case of those who took it in war) or by due process of law, bargain, or purchase, or by allotment. On this principle the lands of Arpinum are said to belong to the Arpinates, the Tusculan lands to the Tusculans; and similar is the assignment of private property. Therefore, inasmuch as in each case some of those things which by nature had been common property became the property of individuals, each one should retain possession of that which has fallen to his lot; and if anyone appropriates to himself anything beyond that, he will be violating the laws of human society.

But since, as Plato has admirably expressed it, we are not born for ourselves alone, but our country claims a share of our being, and our friends a share; and since, as the Stoics hold, everything that the earth produces is created for man's use; and as men, too, are born for the sake of men, that they may be able mutually to help one another; in this direction we ought to follow Nature as our guide, to contribute to the general good by an interchange of acts of kindness, by giving and receiving, thus by our skill, our industry, and our talents to cement human society more closely together, man to man.

The foundation of justice, moreover, is good faith—that is, truth and fidelity to promises and agreements. And therefore we may follow the Stoics, who diligently investigate the etymology of words; and we may accept their statement that "good faith" is so called because what is promised is "made good," although some may find this derivation rather farfetched.

There are, on the other hand, two kinds of injustice—the one, on the part of those who inflict wrong, the other on the part of those who, when they can, do not shield from wrong those upon whom it is being inflicted. For he who, under the influence of anger or some other passion, wrongfully assaults another seems, as it were, to be laying violent hands upon a comrade; but he who does not prevent or oppose wrong, if he can, is just as guilty of wrong as if he deserted his parents or his friends or his country.

*   *   *

But it seems we must trace back to their ultimate sources the principles of fellowship and society that nature has established among men. The first principle is that which is found in the connection subsisting between all the members of the human race; and that bond of connection is reason and speech, which by the processes of teaching and learning, of communicating, discussing, and reasoning associate men together and unite them in a sort of natural fraternity. In no other particular are we farther removed from the nature of beasts; for we admit that they may have courage (horses and lions, for example); but we do not admit that they have justice, equity, and goodness; for they are not endowed with reason or speech.

This, then, is the most comprehensive bond that unites together men as men and all to all; and under it the common right to all things that nature has produced for the common use of man is to be maintained, with the understanding that, while everything assigned as private property by the statutes and by civil law shall be so held as prescribed by those same laws, everything else shall be regarded in the light indicated by the Greek proverb: "Amongst friends all things in common."

II

Justinian, *Institutes* Prooemium, Book 1, Titles 1 and 2 (selections), is reprinted from J. B. Moyle, *The Institutes of Justinian*, by permission of the Clarendon Press, Oxford.

The imperial majesty should be armed with laws as well as glorified with arms, that there may be good government in times both of war and of peace, and the ruler of Rome may not only be victorious over his enemies, but may show himself as scrupulously regardful of justice as triumphant over his conquered foes.

With deepest application and forethought, and by the blessing of God, we have attained both of these objects. The barbarian nations which we have subjugated know our valour, Africa and other provinces without number being once more, after so long an interval, reduced beneath the sway of Rome by victories granted by Heaven, and themselves bearing witness to our dominion. All peoples too are ruled by laws which we have either enacted or arranged. . . .

*　　　　　*　　　　　*

Justice is the set and constant purpose which gives to every man his due. Jurisprudence is the knowledge of things divine and human, the science of the just and the unjust.

The precepts of the law are these: to live honestly, to injure no one, and to give every man his due. The study of law consists of two branches, law public, and law private. The former relates to the welfare of the Roman State; the latter to the advantage of the individual citizen. Of private law then we may say that it is of threefold origin, being collected from the precepts of nature, from those of the law of nations, or from those of the civil law of Rome.

*   *   *

The law of nature is that which she has taught all animals; a law not peculiar to the human race, but shared by all living creatures, whether denizens of the air, the dry land, or the sea. Hence comes the union of male and female, which we call marriage; hence the procreation and rearing of children, for this is a law by the knowledge of which we see even the lower animals are distinguished. The civil law of Rome, and the law of all nations, differ from each other thus. The laws of every people governed by statutes and customs are partly peculiar to itself, partly common to all mankind. Those rules which a state enacts for its own members are peculiar to itself, and are called civil law: those rules prescribed by natural reason for all men are observed by all peoples alike, and are called the law of nations. Thus the laws of the Roman people are partly peculiar to itself, partly common to all nations; a distinction of which we shall take notice as occasion offers. Whenever we speak, however, of civil law, without any qualification, we mean our own; exactly as, when "the poet" is spoken of, without addition or qualification, the Greeks understand the great Homer, and we understand Vergil. But the law of nations is common to the whole human race; for nations have settled certain things for themselves as occasion and the necessities of human life required. For instance, wars arose, and then followed captivity and slavery, which are contrary to the law of nature; for by the law of nature all men from the beginning were born free. The law of nations again is the source of almost all contracts; for instance, sale, hire, partnership, deposit, loan for consumption, and very many others.

Our law is partly written, partly unwritten, as among the Greeks. The written law consists of statutes, plebiscites, senatusconsults, enactments of the Emperors, edicts of the magistrates, and answers of those learned in the law. The unwritten law is that which usage has approved: for ancient customs, when approved by consent of those who follow them, are like statute. And this division of the civil law into two kinds seems not inappropriate, for it appears to have originated in the institutions of

vo states, namely Athens and Lacedaemon; it having been usual in the
latter to commit to memory what was observed as law, while the Athe-
ians observed only what they had made permanent in written statutes.

But the laws of nature, which are observed by all nations alike, are
established, as it were, by divine providence, and remain ever fixed and
immutable: but the municipal laws of each individual state are subject
to frequent change, either by the tacit consent of the people, or by the
subsequent enactment of another statute.

Index